Costs and Statistics: Basic Cost Principles, Mapping Out the Cost System, Graphs and Statistics, Expense Control

A.W. Shaw Company

COSTS
AND STATISTICS

BASIC COST PRINCIPLES
MAPPING OUT THE COST SYSTEM
GRAPHS AND STATISTICS
EXPENSE CONTROL

A. W. SHAW COMPANY
CHICAGO   NEW YORK
LONDON

COSTS
AND STATISTICS

BASIC COST PRINCIPLES
MAPPING OUT THE COST SYSTEM
GRAPHS AND STATISTICS
EXPENSE CONTROL

A. W. SHAW COMPANY
CHICAGO   NEW YORK
LONDON

CONTENTS

I—PLANNING YOUR COST SYSTEM

II—FINDING AND RECORDING COSTS

III—COST SYSTEMS THAT PROVED EFFECTIVE

CONTENTS

IV—USING GRAPHS AND STATISTICS IN BUSINESS

SPECIAL ILLUSTRATIONS

PART I—PLANNING
YOUR COST SYSTEM

Take Your Problem to Pieces

SEEK out the facts of a case and the conclusions are usually self-evident.

Many failures are caused by lack of thorough analysis because those responsible are "too busy" to investigate.

Practically every subject can be dissected and analyzed.

In this way errors and waste are reduced and economic saving made and differences of opinion avoided.

Analyze your own problems; if the subject can afford the outlay, have a special department for this purpose.

Cultivate a conscious, reasoning analysis of your own work. It is easily acquired and its persistent application rapidly develops its usefulness.

John S. Lawrence

CALIFORNIA

JOHN S. LAWRENCE

Of Lawrence & Company

I

FINDING THE COST FACTS IN YOUR BUSINESS

By Neil M. Clark

I BELIEVE we can make that sheet iron pipe ourselves cheaper than we can get it outside," said the foreman of a sheet metal shop making a special line of work.

It was the dull season of the year, and the manager told him to go ahead on an order that was just ready to go to another concern. They made it a test lot. The shop had a thorough cost system, and every item of expense entering into the manufacture was carefully recorded. When the foreman came to discuss final results with the manager, they found that the total cost of the home-made product was a fraction less than what they had been paying outside.

"It's up to you," said the manager. "You can have all future orders. And see how much you can beat this first record."

The foreman appreciated the system which made it possible for him to know his costs, and so keep his men busy in a season ordinarily slack, at the same time serving the firm by affording them a considerable economy in materials. This is only one of numerous economies arrived at in this shop by the use of an effective cost system.

A good cost system is a telescope which brings every

activity of your business to a sharp focus, and makes the abnormal items, wastes and mistakes, stand out in relief to catch your eye. It keeps a record of raw material; it keeps track of men—the work they do and the work they ought to do; it tells the condition of every article and job in the factory; it automatically points out where wastes are occurring and what you must do to stop them. A real cost system explains past results, and forms a guide for the future conduct of your business, furnishing a basis on which to make prices, or cut them intelligently to meet competition. You have this information at once, when the leaks are commencing; not months afterwards, when they have had time to grow large and drain off your profits.

A cost system does these positive things; it also gives indirect results. The purchasing agent has a check on his material and a system which brings to light the true and false economies of his purchases. The employees all down the line are constantly on the watch to stop leaks, because they know the results of their work are the basis of daily and monthly comparisons in your office. The salesman on the road knows which of the lines in his sample case bring a big profit, and which sell at a small margin. Instead of working in haphazard fashion, every member of the organization from your desk to the day laborer is working on an assured basis of facts.

Your selling price, by which the buying public largely measures you, is made up of the three big elements: Factory Cost, Selling Cost and Profit. An undertaking may be very efficiently organized in the making or selling end, and yet not prove a success, because gains in one department are offset by losses in another. It is, therefore, essential to know what your office helpers and salesmen are costing you, and clip down wastes in the distributing organization, as well as to know precisely what you are paying for labor, power or material in the factory itself.

The ideal of cost keeping is to connect all classes' of expenditure with the items on which they are incident. Even the smallest plant, however, finds it impossible to

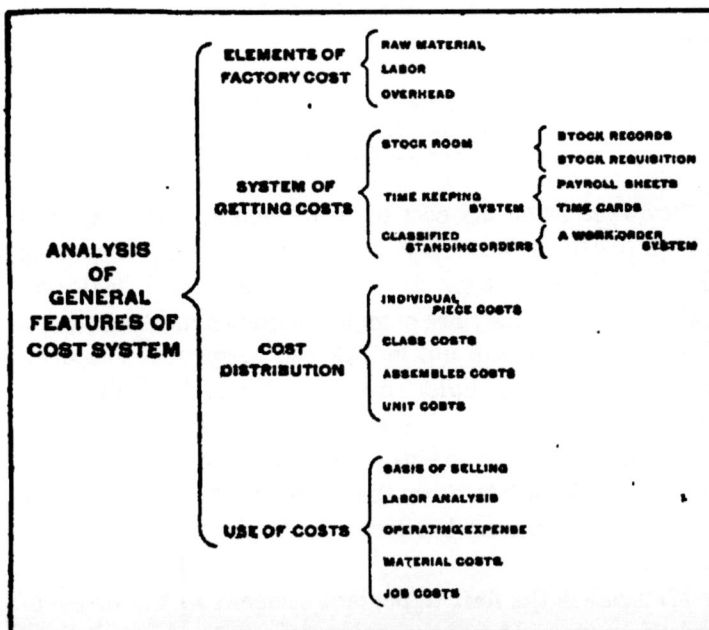

FIGURE I: *This chart outlines the essential features of any cost system, giving the relation between the items which enter into the cost of manufacture and showing the specific means by which facts are collected*

trace every expenditure to its exact source, to determine which job shall carry the burden of the cigar given by the superintendent to a prospective customer. And even if it were possible, the time and pains spent would not be repaid. It is easy to go too much into details in getting costs when once you become fascinated with the idea of allocating every expenditure.

Common sense rules the installation of a cost system as much as anything else. Make the system fit your business. Do not stop every other leak and ruin yourself collecting top-heavy cost statistics. Ask, first of all, what facts you need to know; and then devise a system that will get those facts for you in the best and simplest form possible.

MATERIAL *and direct labor charges are cost elements which can be apportioned accurately to the job or specific work on which they are incident.*

Two factors of the cost of a finished article can, with a high degree of accuracy, be charged to the job causing them. These factors are direct labor and material. Taken together they are commonly known as Prime Cost. The items which can not be charged to specific jobs comprise power, heat, light and rent, taxes, insurance, depreciation, interest on investment, repairs or upkeep, indirect labor, miscellaneous items, and the proportion of office expense allotted to the factory. These items are variously known as burden, overhead, or running expenses.

Material is the first important element in the order of manufacture. If a mechanic came into your factory office and asked for seventy-five cents, you would demand a detailed explanation of his reasons, and record the amount on your books with religious care. Do you exercise the same care when he goes to the stock room and demands material?

In cost terms, material includes only that which becomes a physical part of the finished product. A scaffold built to assist in the construction of a machine is not technically material, especially if the planks and spikes can be used for succeeding jobs. Wastes and petty thefts of material are very liable to occur, but a little care in devising a satisfactory stock room system serves to stop the leaks and make this item a definite charge against the job into which it goes.

The stock room clerk is in charge of all stores and you should hold him responsible for the proper handling of them. The first essential is a stock record, which may, with advantage, take the form of a perpetual stock inventory. Each kind of material has its own card, on which the stockkeeper enters the amounts as they are received from time to time. He issues material only when a requisition properly filled out and signed by a responsible party in the department concerned (generally the foreman) is presented to him. He records on his stock inventory card the amount issued, and makes the charge to the proper department and job.

Whenever any material is not used on the job for which it was originally intended, or is diverted to another department, your system should provide means by which the stockkeeper receives a record of the fact, in order that no job may be charged with more material than has actually entered into it. Waste can generally be sold and will bring in a small amount to offset the loss.

Your chief ally in cutting down the leaks in material is the workman himself. Teach him to realize that you are constantly relying upon him and measuring his efficiency, not only by the amount of work which he turns out, but also by the percentage of wasted material charged against him, and your account with wasted material will rapidly decrease.

Direct labor is the second element which can be ac-

curately charged to the proper job. Time clocks record
the time of the arrival and departure of employees with
more fairness and accuracy than a timekeeper can or
will attain. In addition to the time clock it is essential
to have a system of time cards on which the number of
hours spent by each workman on each job or class of
work is recorded. Checked against one another and analyzed in the cost department, these records furnish complete statistics of the time spent in direct labor on a particular product. Reduce this to terms of money, and you
have the direct labor cost. If you have established a
standard cost, you can tell at a glance whether the work
was done with more or less than ordinary efficiency. If
it compares poorly with former records, instant investigation should show the reason. Here is one of the places
where a good cost system should prove its value as a
check on wasteful expenditures.

The costs of direct labor and material are fairly easy
to ascertain. But burden is the crux of cost systems,.
the rock on which many of them split. Not that it is
much harder to find the total amount of the incidental
factory expense than the total of wages and material,
but the difficulty comes in distributing this amount
equitably over the product when it is found, so that
each job shall bear its proper weight of cost.

Manufacturing plants differ so widely that it is impossible to have a "one best way" of burden distribution
for every trade and every plant. Conditions vary and
the peculiar circumstances of your factory will determine
whether you apportion burden according to the number
of direct labor hours or according to the amount of
wages paid for this direct labor; whether you will fix
machine rates to be charged hourly against every job
using the machines, or, finally, whether you decide on a

refinement of one or more of these methods.

Most manufacturers find either the productive hour plan or the percentage on wages plan detailed and yet simple enough to meet their needs. The former takes the number of direct labor hours as the basis of distribution; the latter, the amount of direct labor wages. Assume, for instance, that in a certain factory employing two hundred men, the total number of direct labor hours for the month of March is forty thousand, and the full amount of wages paid for this direct labor is $10,000. The total burden for the month amounts to $9,000. Job number thirty-seven is the construction of a heavy machine. The direct labor spent on it amounts to three thousand hours, with a direct labor wage of $900. The material entering into the machine amounts to $1,000. What, according to the two plans outlined above, will be the total Factory Cost of the job?

D ISTRIBUTING *overhead charges so that each kind or piece of work bears its due proportion is essential in right cost accounting—the four methods.*

Consider first the productive hour plan. The total amount to be distributed is $9,000. The total number of direct labor hours worked during the month is forty thousand, giving a charge of $0.225 to be charged against every job for the number of direct labor hours spent on it. Worked out for job number thirty-seven, this gives the following results:

Material $1,000
Wages 900
Burden (3,000 hrs. x .225)........... 675
_____

Total Factory Cost..................$2,575

When you distribute the burden by the percentage on

wages plan results differ considerably. The amount to
be distributed remains the same, but it is distributed on
the basis of the $10,000 spent for direct wages. Burden
being $9,000, you have to add to the cost 90% of direct
wages to account for burden. The results follows:

Material $1,000
Wages 900
Burden (900 x .90).................. 810
                                   _____
Total Factory Cost $2,710

A difference of $135 due to different methods, and
the question immediately arises, which is more accurate?

If your factory employs a large number of men receiving about the same rate of pay, the hourly burden
plan is more accurate. If, on the other hand, your workmen range from skilled mechanics to truck-haulers at
$9 a week and your pay roll is greatly diversified, the
percentage-on-wages plan will distribute the burden more
satisfactorily. For the average shop, especially at the
beginning, the percentage plan is the simplest and most
practicable.

The machine rate plan is designed to meet the needs
of factories which maintain a number of expensive machines, where the labor charge is comparatively unim-
portant. Under this plan each machine assumes a portion of the total burden according to the amount of
space it occupies, the amount of light, heat and power it
uses, a proportion of the expense of supervision, and so
on. This amount is divided by the full number of hours
which the shop runs. The resulting hourly rate is
charged against every job using the machine. Thus,
suppose the piece of machinery whose manufacture was
considered above, required use of three machines, A, B,
and C, with hourly rates of $0.152, $0.124 and $0.21 re-

spectively, and four hundred hours were spent on machine A, one thousand hours on machine B, and twelve hundred hours on machine C. In that case, the cost of the machine, figured on a machine-rate basis would be as follows:

Material	$1,000.00
Wages	900.00
Machine A (400x0.152)	60.80
Machine B (1,000x0.124)	124.00
Machine C (1,200x0.21)	252.00
Total Factory Cost	$2,336.80

It is at once apparent that the machine rate fails to take into consideration time when the machine lies idle. If every machine were running full time, the plan would be almost perfect; but stoppages for repairs or other reasons are unavoidable. The percentage of idle time is not large in the average well-managed shop, but in some cases delays are numerous and large, and then this unconsidered and unapportioned burden may become an item of serious importance.

Attempting to overcome this difficulty, the scientific machine rate plan is theoretically as nearly perfect as any plan of apportionment can be; but practically, except for large or complex shops, it may prove too involved to be of great service.

Under this plan, the shop is divided into a number of production centers, each of which is a machine with its operator, or the bench of a handworker. Each center pays rent, and assumes all other charges which it can by analysis properly be made to bear, independently of what is paid by other production centers. This forms a charge which is apportioned to every job on an hourly rate. All items, including those which are allocated to production centers as well as those which are not, are gathered together in a monthly shop charge account, which is simply the total amount of burden. The difference between this and the amount charged to specific jobs is distributed as a supplementary rate over the product of the shop by any desired plan: hourly burden, or percentage on wages, as you choose. The ratio of this supplementary rate to the amount charged against jobs by the machine rate is, from month to month, a varying barometer of the shop's efficiency. In theory the plan, as a refinement on the machine rate plan, is ideal; in practice you may find it unnecessary to make so completely accurate a distribution.

MARKETING *an article may cost as much or more than making it—finding the exact amount of this item and charging it to the proper class of work.*

Up to this point we have considered only the cost incurred in laying the article at the shipping-room door ready for distribution. Selling Cost is a large additional item which must be added to Factory Cost to secure the total Cost to Make and Sell. Its amount varies greatly in different businesses. Some organizations have a large force of salesmen and conduct expensive advertising campaigns. Others are so situated that they do no advertising, have few salesmen or none at all, and conduct their selling with a minimum of correspondence. In one case, selling cost may be more than 100% of Factory Cost; in the other it may not be more than 10%. The simplest and most practical method of distributing Selling Cost is on the basis of Factory Cost.

If for example the total cost of a certain product in the shop is $10,000 for the month of March, and the total selling cost is $1,000, 10% of the factory cost of each article represents the proportion of selling cost it must bear. One article, however, may actually cost again as much as another to sell, though the factory cost of both is nearly the same. In the shop manufacturing a variety of articles, therefore, it is customary to classify the objects with an approximation at the actual amount it costs to put them on the market. Thus, in the above case, one class of machine might require to have 20% added to its Factory Cost to represent the amount expended in selling it; while in the case of another kind of

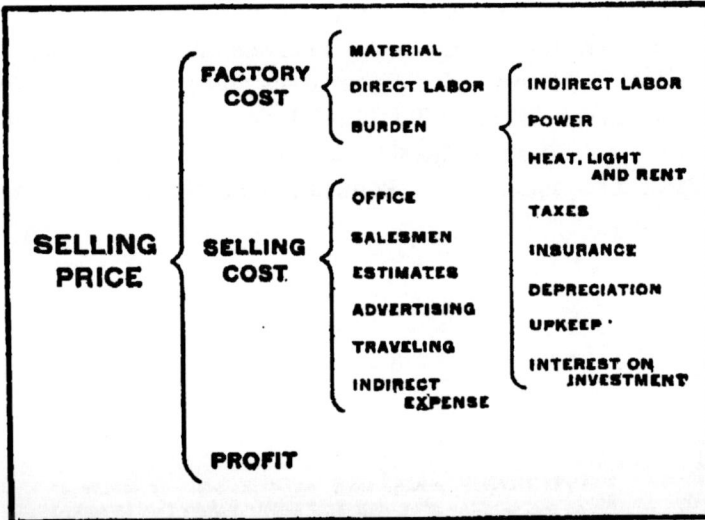

FIGURE II: *Selling price is made up of the three big factors: cost to make, cost to sell, and profit. This chart shows the elements that enter into each factor*

article the percentage of selling expense—owing to its being a staple and requiring a minimum of advertising and salesmanship—might fall to as low as three or four per cent of its factory cost.

The difference between the total cost of any article, which may be called the Cost to Make and Sell, and the final selling price is profit; or if the margin runs the other way, loss.

Your cost system tells you what you must know about your business to conduct it on a basis of profit and efficiency. It gives you a record of and check on all materials and supplies, it furnishes a record of the day's work of each producing workman, tells where he worked and what he accomplished; it divides with as much accuracy as is possible or necessary the general expense, placing the burden where it belongs; it forms, finally, the basis for an intelligent analysis and comparison of all units of cost. Know your costs and you have in hand the means of stopping blind leaks, of cutting off unprofitable lines of goods and meeting competition in a fair and square way, knowing precisely what you are doing.

EFFICIENCY *means keen self-criticism. It means to go out into the shop and find nothing there that is sacred or fixed. It means that in that shop six months ago shall be ancient history. It means the dropping of tradition, the forgetting of ghosts, the questioning of everything. It means the old Scripture doctrine, "Prove all things. Hold fast that which is good," and only that.*

—William C. Redfield
Secretary of Commerce

II

MAKING WORKMEN PARTNERS IN COST CUTTING

By Vernon Hoxie
Vice-President, Peerless Wire Fence Company

WHEN I was serving my apprenticeship at a mechanic's bench, we thought our employer had a perfect cost system, for it took the time of two clerks and required more than a score of bewildering forms and cards. Its operation was an impressive ceremony—so far removed from our conception that we supposed, of course, it must be good. Workmen who were responsible for wastes in material and labor did not understand the method of keeping records and locating leakages. And now I doubt if the manager knew much more. Once a month he would storm about the high cost of manufacture, but he would not point out specifically where the costs were running up or why. From my later experience as a factory executive I know that his cost system, like many others, was inefficient because production costs were not rightly distributed and because the men who were responsible for production did not understand the application of the system and how it touched them.

A cost system that is actually going to cut down costs must show precisely where wastes of material and labor are occurring and provide some means for checking them at once. And it must be so simple that every employee can understand it and know just how his mistakes will show up in the final figures.

But a cost system will not cut down costs. All it can do is to show you where to use the pruning-knife. This I do by taking my foremen and employees into my confidence. When Harry K—is promoted from a loom to foreman of a weaving room I call him into my office and we get together.

"It's up to me, Harry," I tell the new foreman, "to produce the best fence at the lowest cost, and I want you to help me do it."

Then with sample time sheets, repair tickets and requisition slips I show him just how the timekeeper makes up the cost records for each day. When the new foreman leaves my desk he has a good idea of the importance of figures and how his work out there in the weaving room will be reduced to cold hard net facts each night.

FREQUENT meeting and daily contact with foremen by the executive puts the men on guard to find hidden leaks and time-saving methods in their work.

By distributing the production among the weaving rooms and looms it has been possible to stimulate competition between men of the various rooms. When a loom breaks or a wire snarls, the foreman is sure to let me know at once (each department has a 'phone) why the day's work will show a shortage. If reports were made monthly the average might show up all right, but the smallest delay looms up in the daily report. Knowing this, the foreman and workers are alike more anxious to get the machine running again as soon as possible, and by having the trouble reported at once I am in a position to render assistance if it be needed.

During the day I have conferences with my foremen in the office and in their departments. They are free to come to me at any time or any place. There is absolute harmony between us, and I encourage the men to look upon me as only a fellow worker in the production of wire fence. But I am convinced that our whole co-

DAILY TIME REPORT SHEET

MACHINE SHOP, BLACKSMITH SHOP, DIE ROOM AND PATTERN ROOM

NAME _____ NO. _____

_____ 191 ___

STATE HERE THE KIND OF WORK YOU   HOURS
HAVE BEEN DOING

TOTAL HOURS _____

NOTE: EACH KIND OF WORK MUST BE ITEMIZED

O. K. _____ FOREMAN

FORM I: A daily time report sheet like this is filled out at night by every employee and given to the timekeeper, who compares the figures with the time clock records

operative cost system has been built and held together in the bi-monthly meetings of all the foremen.

This is probably the most important feature of our system. While it may appear to be far removed from a cost system, I have proved to my own satisfaction that it bears the closest relation to cutting costs and increasing the production efficiency of individuals and departments. The men come over to the factory in the evening for the session. We gather around a big table and turn the meeting into a social and business affair. Everything is so absolutely informal that every man feels like coming right out with his troubles—and experience shows that he actually does so.

Jim Brown, Foreman of Warehouse B, for instance, tells us that he believes it is costing too much to get the wire into a certain switch. Immediately we consider the problem and try to draw out a suggestion for cutting down the cost. The foreman of Loom Room 3 is having trouble with a certain loom, and he tells us about that. Probably the foreman of one of the other rooms has been up against this same problem and he tells his fellow worker how to get around the trouble. Thus another cost is cut.

I know that these meetings and the whole general co-operative spirit which exists among the men pay our factory in decreased costs, for some of our biggest money-saving policies and operations have been created or suggested at these meetings. At one of these meetings our head draftsman suggested the idea of the telpher or monorail system for handling wire. Little did any one think when he suggested it that the idea would materialize into the longest overhead transportation system of its kind in the world. The worth of this suggestion is given particular significance as a cost cutting element when it is known that this system paid for itself in two years, and that it saves us forty per cent of the former cost of handling our finished product.

At another cost-cutting conference the machine shop foreman suggested a form of automatic releasing grapples for handling the fence in connection with the telpher system. Two months ago, the assistant superintendent suggested a wire guide—a simple casting, but an improvement which holds the warp wires of the fence firmly in position to receive the tie or locking wire, and enables us to speed up the looms, and thus make 20 per cent more fence a day.

Every meeting contributes some item that cuts down the cost. But even if these meetings did not produce one suggestion, they would be justified by the spirit of cooperation which they have built up, and this spirit of cooperation has passed further down the line to the employees working for these various foremen.

The details of the cost system necessarily differ with each line of industry, but the principle is of universal

STOCK ROOM

_____ 191 ____

DELIVER TO BEARER THE FOLLOWING
MATERIAL TO BE CHARGED TO _____

NO. _____ IN LOOM ROOM NO. _____   _____ FOREMAN

NO.		FROM BIN NO.

ABOVE MATERIAL ISSUED BY _____

FORM II: The stock room reports on a form like this the amount of material issued to each department. These reports also go to the timekeeper, who records the cost in time

application — the ultimate way to cut costs is through men. For unless they understand and see clearly how everything they do or fail to do affects the production, the costs cannot be cut to the bone.

A cost system is absolutely essential to every manufacturing business. In experimenting with our cost system, we have concluded that it should have two features: it should be so simple that any employee can understand it and should furnish the production manager with daily, or at least weekly reports of production by departments.

SIMPLICITY *is the first essential of good cost system; thoroughness is the second—finding the facts promptly and in detail saves many wastes.*

The first feature enables the executive to point out to his foremen the reason for his orders and secures active coöperation in cutting down costs in every department. The second feature gives the executive daily and weekly bulletins of this production. An error today is rectified tomorrow. It doesn't eat up profits for a month before being discovered.

Our cost system is so simple that the timekeeper makes it up in his spare time, and every foreman understands its operation. It furnishes me with daily bulletins that are the basis of my day-to-day supervision. The records of the previous day's work which are laid on my desk each morning enable me to keep my hand on the pulse of every department.

The daily costs of manufacture are made from workmen's time sheets, repair tickets and requisitions in the stock room. At the end of each day every employee must fill out a daily time report sheet (Form I). These are handed to the foremen and then to the timekeeper, who compares them next day with the clock records for the purpose of verifying the time consumed.

In the meantime the timekeeper has received from the stock room all the requisitions (Form II) for material issued from the various departments for the previous day. From the machine shop come all repair tickets. The machine shop is run as if a separate institution. When some department requires the services of a machinist, the foreman issues an order on the machine shop, and the machinist's services are charged against this department.

As soon as the timekeeper has received all the time

FORM III: *This is the form of requisition given to the stock room. The stockkeeper reports each evening to the timekeeper what stock has been issued to each department*

sheets, repair tickets and requisitions, he spreads these upon an analysis sheet (Form IV) which distributes the costs of manufacturing the previous day's fence into twelve divisions of fence manufacture. Such costs as oil, waste and general expense are secured from the requisi-

tion slips and charged to the proper department. The
machinery repairs are secured from the job tickets which
the machinist turns in on the completion of each job.

FINDING *leaks means the careful study of accurately,
prepared reports—expense figures bring to light
unnoticed abuses and especially efficient work.*

On the expense report shown for one month, it may be
noted that Loom Room 1, for example, had charged
against it a total of $53.89 for machinery repairs, while
Loom Rooms 2 and 3 had charges for this work of $11.48
and $14.44. Thus the repair work for the day in Loom
Room 1 increased the manufacturing cost to $5.96 per ton
because of the expense of repairs and intermittent idle-
ness of machines. Loom Room 2 with about one-fifth
less repairs turned out nearly five times the work and
consequently had a low cost of manufacture—the price
per ton in this room being $2.05. Loom Room 3 with
$14.44 repairs had a manufacturing cost of $6.17 due to
the fact that this room was manufacturing a narrow
spaced fence on which there is a corresponding increase
in price.

With this report on my desk each afternoon I compare it carefully with the reports of preceding days and
can instantly catch the slightest increase of cost in any
process of manufacture. When I see a big repair bill or
a charge heavier than usual, I get the foreman in charge
on the telephone and learn the reason before he has an
opportunity to duplicate the charge on today's sheet.
The men know that I will see these things, and usually
they beat the report to me and tell me why the cost per
ton is going to be high on the day's expense report. And
this is just what I want them to do, for it shows that
they thoroughly understand and appreciate the applica-

FORM IV (large sheet): On this form cost items are analyzed daily. The information is taken from requisition slips, time sheets and repair tickets. FORM V (smaller sheet): Warehouse expenses are filled out on this report sheet

tion of the system and want to keep down the costs in their departments.

The warehouse expense report is made up from time sheets, repair tickets and requisitions. In addition to the warehouse expense, it shows the daily costs of conducting the machine shop, die room, blacksmith shop, pattern room and such charges as are made under the heads of real estate, general expense and advertising. Charges under these heads and the power plant are apportioned among the proper departments of the business. This sheet is shown in Form V.

How to cut down costs is every factory executive's problem. And the secret lies, not alone in the cost system, but in its application—in getting the workers who are responsible for costs into a coöperative spirit, willing to help each other and straining every point to keep down costs in their individual departments. But this cannot be done unless the system is simple and understandable.

✠

IF a man knows what every article he manufactures costs him to produce, and is absolutely certain that not the most insignificant element of that cost has by any chance been omitted, he is in a position to meet competition and to meet i t closely.

—Alexander H. Revell
President, A. H. Revell Company

III

WHERE TO SAVE IN COST KEEPING

By N. P. Pritchard

Manufacturers who use cost systems may be divided into two classes—those who are afraid of the obvious advantages of a cost system because of the expense it will involve, and those who overdo cost work to an extent which they themselves never realize. The average manufacturer should take the middle ground. You cannot get accurate costs without paying for them, but you must also realize that the cost department can be handled economically just as well as any other department in the factory.

Some men believe that comprehensive costs can only be arrived at by an army of clerks. Others are just as sure that simpler methods and fewer clerks give better and quicker results. After ten years' practice and experience in cost work I believe that the simpler the methods of arriving at costs, the better; the fewer parts, the less liable is the machine to get out of order; and this fact is equally as applicable to the cost office.

To manufacture economically, costs must be known, but how many factory owners know what it costs to get their costs? I have talked with a great many manufacturers and have been surprised to learn that though they wanted correct costs they paid very little attention to the details of their cost department beyond complaining about the excessive expense of its maintenance.

In establishing an economical and accurate cost system the first thing necessary is to fit the system to your business. The organization of the cost department has much to do with the success or failure and the expense of such work. Many systems are inaugurated at a great expense only to be abandoned within a short time because the system runs the factory.

Such is apt to be the case with that second class of manufacturers who overload their business with records. I know of a manufacturer who thought he needed a new system. He wanted to get costs in great detail and to know quickly the cost of doing work in each department. So he called in an outside man who went over the plant and the system then in use. The expert reported that the new system would not cost him more than five thousand dollars to install. This manufacturer's old cost system was really doing satisfactory work. Two hours after a lot of machines were completed the costs were known on every piece, and these costs were surprisingly correct for the amount of clerical help on the work. This cost department consisted of a manager and three clerks. The total wages for the three were sixty dollars a week. It cost about one thousand dollars to install the system.

FITTING *the cost system to the size and needs of the business is essential if it is not to prove top-heavy and more expensive than it is worth.*

But because the owner wanted more detail the expert was engaged and the cost force increased to ten men. It now costs this manufacturer seventy-five cents to find the cost on a twenty-one cent article. Of course, on higher priced goods the proportionate cost of finding the costs is not so obviously wrong.

In building an organization to take care of the cost work of a factory, use care in hiring the man in charge of the cost department. Give him from one hundred and twenty-five dollars to one hundred and fifty dollars a month if your plant employs from four hundred to five hundred men. Let him take a month or two in getting acquainted with factory conditions and so adapt the system he knows about to those conditions. Then after the system is in working order, have him keep it going and make changes which are bound to occur even in the most carefully thought-out system.

I was in a plant some time ago where the attitude of the manager was responsible for the high cost of that department. He wouldn't give the cost man responsibility, with the result that his cost department, he told me, cost him $10,000 a year.

In another shop in the same line of business where the cost manager had a little more to say, the department cost $4,732 per year. If my friend had left his cost manager, who was a very capable man, alone he would have had the same, if not better results, and made a great saving.

At still another plant, the system was changed about as often as the weather, simply because it was not working in about two weeks after it was installed. Here the manner of operating was to put a system on paper and assume that because it worked theoretically, it should be a success the minute it was put to the test.

This firm changed cost managers and systems about four times in a year; its heads are still surprised at how much money they have spent, and how little authentic information they have. The other extreme was a large shop which employed nine hundred men. This shop had every facility for getting out the work, and the various departments were arranged in rotation, so that if the first operation was done on the first floor, you did not have to send work to the top floor for the next operation. The shop was increasing in size and the firm was going to put in a more comprehensive system that would be in keeping with a strictly up-to-the-minute plant. The secretary told me that he did not expect to have the new system in working order for at least six months, and that the firm was perfectly willing that the manager should devote this time to the study of the plant and its particular needs. It simply figured that by so doing it would know exactly what it was about and thereby avoid expensive future changes.

I NSTALLING *a cost accounting system must be gone about gradually, starting first in the stock room and working from there into all departments.*

In my own work I find that the most inexpensive way of installing a cost system is to put it in gradually. Take up the stock rooms first. Are they arranged so that the work, both physical and manual, can be done to best advantage? The facts the stock clerk collects determine the accuracy of your data on the amount of material used.

Here is one of the points where it is well to study what it costs to get costs. One stock clerk can attend to considerable work if the hour or two that is wasted by the stock boys every day is utilized. Stock boys can check the bills, keep the supplies' consumption sheet in order and do other routine work for the stock clerk, who will then have time to devote his attention to keeping up the stock on hand. The better arranged the stock room is the fewer clerks are required and the lower the cost of finding the cost of material.

The cost of handling stock in one shop was cut down, and the number of laborers needed to handle it was greatly reduced, to say nothing of trucking and elevator service. This was taken care of by having a stock room on each floor. These branch stock rooms carried only the material used on this floor for the construction of the machines which these departments built.

The third floor was devoted exclusively to the manufacture of milling machines. All the machinery necessary for the production of the finished article was also located on this floor, with the exception of the planers and automatic screw machines.

When we wanted to build No. 3 millers, all the raw stock was carried up to this department and distributed among the machines. As soon as the parts were completed they were put in this third floor stock room, instead of being hauled downstairs, to be again returned to the third floor when the assemblers were ready for it. The machine gang was always one lot ahead of the assembling gang.

This worked wonders in the way of prompt deliveries, as the finished parts were always ready for assembling. This milling machine department was composed of fifty men. One man kept time, ordered the raw material, and kept the stock room in A-1 condition, and he was minus his left hand.

The stock office is but one branch of the cost department and the more uniformly it is laid out the easier it is to get and handle material and the fewer the clerks required to keep track of it.

The third man to consider in your cost department is the time clerk. Usually the time clerk's position is undervalued. Of all clerical positions in the cost office that of timekeeper is the hardest, and more depends

upon him than on any other man in the force. Where
work is changing continually one timekeeper to every
one hundred men is about the limit of capacity. I would
rather have one too many than one short, because any
spare time a surplus man may have may be used to
advantage by a cost manager who is a good executive.
The timekeeper should know the products, have a fair
idea as to what operations are necessary to complete a
piece and about how long each operation should take.

M ECHANICAL *devices in the timekeeping department do much to save the cost of clerical labor and
help to speed up the machinery of cost-finding.*

The time-keeping department is one of the most important in assembling costs and ought to be studied carefully. In one factory time is saved by giving parts and
operations numbers instead of names. The time clerk
does not have to write on the form, "J. Adams, boring
twenty-four-inch head cap;" he writes instead, the
man's check-number, No. 40, operation No. 3, part H 2,
in which designation H stands for the size of the machine on which No. 2 the head cap is to be used. This
method not only makes a more legible card, but it takes
about a third as long to write.

When I first started a time system through the shop,
the time was marked on Forms I and II; Form I was
used for machine work and Form II for the assembling.
There were two objections to this, however. First, two
cards for the same machines meant double work with a
chance of having some of the Form II cards lost.

The other objection was caused by not being able to
compute the time or cost until the job had been completed, as the card had to remain with the work until
the last machine operation had been completed and then

CASTING TAG

NO.	FOR	AMOUNT	FOREMAN NOTIFIED	DELIVERED	PATTERN TIME

NAME

DRAWING NO.

DATE

NO. DATE

PATTERN NO.

DATE	OPERATION	DEPT. NO.	JIG NO.	TOOLS NEEDED	TIME ALLOW-ANCE	WK. NO.	START	STOP	TOTAL TIME EACH	LEAVE DEPT.	ADDITIONAL INFORMATION	WK. NO.	START	STOP

AMOUNT

NAME

WK. NO. RATE

ORDER NO.	PIECE NO.	OPERATION	START	STOP	TOTAL HOURS

DATE HOUR DATE HOUR

ASSEMBLING

CHECK NO. DATE

PIECE	START	STOP	TOTAL

PTN. NO.

WEIGHT

FRMN. NOTIFIED

REMARKS

FORMS I and II: *A machine shop used the larger blank (FORM I) for machine work, and the front card (FORM II) for assembling work. This duplication of clerical and filing labor was done away with by devising one efficient card, the center one, FORM III* it followed the work to the stock room, where it was inspected and the number of rejected parts marked on the card. Only after this stage was the card allowed away from the work.

These objections were overcome by using Form III. The original time card (Form I) was made smaller, but it displayed the information in a much more compact and usable shape. The new time card was made out each day, and for each man, by the personal notation of the timekeeper, but it could have been done equally as well by time stamps.

Every night these cards were sent to the office and checked against the clock slips the first thing in the morning, after which they were entered on the comparative cost card.

By adopting these cards instead of the old ones we were able to know the cost and time on every job in the shop as it progressed, and as the time was distributed on the comparative cost, cards at once, it was not necessary to have files for the keeping of the originals. It cut out the two cards, and made time-keeping easier and quicker, besides cutting in half the clerical work in the office.

Only a careful study of the cost department and the work of a good cost man will develop little short cuts like these, which will tend to reduce the cost of getting costs. Probably a saving in the cost department can be made in the office where the time, expense and material are distributed on the various jobs. I have found by actual test that a girl with a calculating machine cannot be beaten as a cost clerk. Her records are more reliable, neater and more conscientious than those made by the average man. It has been proved that a girl and a machine can do as much as three men at a salary of

one man, and in some cases the clerical work can be done
for half what it would cost to pay an ordinary clerk.
The girl will operate a machine ten hours a day for
sixteen dollars a week and do the work of three men.

L ITTLE *savings which prevent big losses can be
made in the cost office as well as in other departments of a business—efficiency, not size, counts.*

If the factory is large enough to have two clerks besides the cost manager in the office it is advisable to have
one of the clerks familiar with the typewriter. One
adding machine operator made a saving in handling
records of sixty per cent the first year in one factory
and by spreading the cost of the machine with an
allowance for repairs and an allowance of six per cent
on the investment, it costs eight cents a day to own a
machine in the office. It is a valuable cost reducer.

In getting the total cost of maintaining a cost department, the final result depends upon the size of the plant,
but whatever the size of the plant, the first year's costs
will be higher than that of the succeeding year. Generally it will run from one thousand to two thousand
dollars higher. This expense is largely brought about by
the changes which have to be made, condensing in this
place, enlarging in another. It is impossible to avoid
entirely this increase of the first year's expense, but it
can be brought to a minimum by going slow and considering every detail from every angle.

A good cost system consists of a series of units so
closely cemented together that to an outsider they appear as one. To operate a cost department satisfactorily
the man in charge must be a good executive. He ought
not to have much actual clerical work to do because his
value and the value of the cost department depend not

so much on the actual keeping of the records as in pointing out the records that show how costs can be reduced.

A cost department is unquestionably an expense. It
does not make so much difference how little or how
much it costs, but as an expense it must be charged over
each job. This should not interfere with getting some
kind of an idea of how long it takes a clerk to do his
work and if the cost department is studied with the idea
of reducing the cost of getting costs a great saving can
be made.

Take forms and blanks as a sample of what can be
done in reducing costs. One manager wanted a form
drawn up which would show him the amount of time
each job took, the cost of material and the total cost on
every piece and every machine that was manufactured.
He talked the matter over with the chief draftsman and
the superintendent; thought it was impossible to get
out a sheet for every size and class of machine, but a
little study of what was required, and a classification of
some of the details resulted in getting all this information on a sheet eight and one-half by eleven inches.

Under each component part were headings for each
part of the machine. A space was left for any changes
made through a change in design or special features.
These changes were added in by hand. Three sheets of
this sort were sufficient to contain complete records of
each machine. These sheets were made of the standard form and printed in lots of one thousand. A little
thought had cut the printer's bill seventy-five per cent,
to say nothing of the time and bother of keeping track
of different conditions and classes of machines.

It is the handling of little details like these that de-
cides in good measure how much your cost department
will cost. The whole cost question can be summed up

as follows: Honestly study your own costs, and then face the truth. Hire a good man, show that you have confidence in him, and pay enough to make enthusiasm worth while. Have it generally understood in the shop and office that his word goes. Many a money-saving idea has been killed by foremen, because it did not suit their convenience. Coöperation does more to cut the cost of costs than anything else. Of course, the number of clerks that you have in the cost department largely depends on how much information you desire to get. In a shop of five hundred men, one stock clerk, two time clerks, two clerks in the office, and a cost manager are ample.

A T THE *desk of the chief executive there must be focused in compact form the substance of all the factors entering production. By this means alone can the factory output be regulated and the most efficient use be made of men, materials and machinery.*

—Edward T. Runge

Factory Organizer and Cost Accountant

IV

MANAGING A COST SYSTEM

By J. M. Butler

SITTING in the office of one of his clients, a consulting accountant listened while the president of a Northern company told him the details of a branch business in Mississippi for which he desired a cost system. The Northern company manufactured limestone building cement, while the Southern industry made cotton cloth of a coarse texture for the bags in which the cement was packed, as well as a finer weave of goods for the market.

As the general features of the industry were outlined, the accountant followed carefully, forming his plan for a system as he learned each new detail. At the end of the consultation he had his system well in mind. As an afterthought, however, the president casually remarked:

"By the way, it is a peculiar fact that it costs more to weave short staple cotton than long staple. Different and better machines have to be used, in spite of the fact that the finished product is not so good."

This casual statement made necessary a complete change in the accountant's plans for a factory system. He had not counted on this factor of differing costs of production for different kinds of raw material. He saw instantly that the cost system he had planned would need to be fundamentally altered to meet a condition which the owner of the business thought insignificant.

Little details like this often throw what seem to be perfectly devised cost systems off the track after a few weeks or months. To devise a satisfactory system for your particular business, you must take into consideration every detail of manufacture, or somewhere you will run into a snag. You cannot devise cost systems on cut and dried plans.

R EVISING *cost systems by "rule of thumb" methods is one reason why some of them fail—no two plants are exactly alike in all their requirements.*

Failure of systems to work once they are installed is a not infrequent complaint, and the reasons are threefold: first, they are improperly devised; second, they are operated by incompetent employees; third, they are supervised by incompetent owners.

Many so-called system devisers have a "rule of thumb" plan for the routine of a cost system. They go to a pigeon hole or cabinet, pull out an envelope, and the system is perfected. They employ a few good bookkeepers or chartered accountants, and give them some lessons on how to conduct their particular cost finding machinery. In a short time the systems die a natural death, or receive a thorough revision from someone having more common sense than undigested theory.

More systems fail through incompetent devisers than through any other one cause. It is absurd to presume that a graduate from a business college or correspondence school can take a few lessons from an accountant and then devise and install a good cost system. He must have practical experience as well as theory.

To that theory and practice must be added, as in all affairs, brains and judgment. A case in point. A young man for a number of years made up cost sheets for a large corporation. He filled them in with figures up to a certain point, and then forwarded them to the general office where they were finished. The young man, having a slight knowledge of bookkeeping, thought he was a cost accountant, so he left his position. His employer charitably gave him a letter lauding his ability, and he branched out for himself. After taking a few lessons from an accountant he then modeled all of his work upon the one small phase of cost keeping which he had been doing all his life. Naturally, his systems failed miserably except in cases where they were rescued by real experts.

Other kinds of "systematizers" are more interested in the sale of stationery and supplies than in the actual efficiency of their systems. They often place such high prices upon their work that few concerns can afford to pay for more than a hurried examination of their business. The result is that they attempt to do in a week what should take months, and create a system that may be correct in general outline but lacks some important detail. Eventually the firm must either pay for an expert's services to straighten matters out, or the system is branded as no good and thrown out.

Chief among the faults of cost systems are their complicated appearance and the high cost of installing and maintaining them. These faults are common among systems installed by men who are theorists only. They talk glibly of "production and non-production hours," "burden," and other technical phrases, but their schemes are not always practical. Here is a case in point.

A large furniture factory bought a high-priced system, including nearly one hundred forms, numerous binders, books and files. The explanation of their use, in typewritten form, made a volume in itself. In sheer desperation the firm employed the deviser at a high salary as auditor so that they could get the system to work. The auditor, at great expense and labor, finally exhibited his costs to the sales manager, who was a thoroughly practical man and told the auditor frankly that the costs were wrong—and proved it to him.

In another case a musical instrument maker was willing to pay for a cost accountant's time at a specified salary if he could get results. He was successful in collecting costs but he added so much expense in clerical help and stationery that the employer balked.

In neither of the above cases did common sense rule. The devising experts in each case got the rates they demanded. But, as they guaranteed results only when they installed their systems at their regular rates they were content with failure. Such incidents bring accountants and systems generally under condemnation, whereas, if the buyer had been wise, or the seller honest, there would have been no failure in either instance.

H*OSTILITY of employees, or their incompetence, may ruin a well-devised system—their sympathetic help must be secured in order to obtain results.*

When a system is once installed incompetent employees may kill it, no matter how well devised it is. Very often the system proves too complicated for them, and often there is some other reason why they are not able to handle it properly.

When you put in a cost system you may antagonize two men; one is the head bookkeeper, the other the factory superintendent. The first receives the impression that he is thought incompetent or he would have arrived at some cost system himself. He is naturally unwilling to admit his inability, so he tries to prove the new system unsuitable or even harmful.

If he is an old and faithful employee, perhaps you are inclined to take his word in preference to that of the hired accountant, and the verdict that "the system is no good," "it won't work," "it is too complicated," or "too expensive," is the result. In time, the bookkeeper works out some system or you go back to guessing the costs. If a superintendent or foreman is incompetent, or if he is negligent and careless, he is very apt to muddle up reports so that no cost accountant can get accurate figures on which to base his work. In either case, if you value his word highly enough, the system is a failure.

As an example in point a large corporation was using a perpetual inventory system and it was compelled, at the end of its fiscal year, to write off $250,000 to loss because the ledger showed material on hand valued at that amount. As a matter of fact, there was no such material on hand. The cost man had based his sheets on reports sent in by the superintendent; he saw that they were wrong and called attention to them from time to time. No heed was given to him, however, and finally he was discharged by his department and the superintendent promoted by his superior officer. This instance shows incompetence in both employee and employer.

The average owner knows little about the details of the work in his accounting department. Proof of this is found in the daily failures in every kind of business. If owners knew even approximately the cost of manufacturing, they could better judge whether to go into business or stay out. The average man puts money into a business proposition that looks good at first glance. Only too often he overlooks some vital consideration. He is perhaps too "economical" to employ a competent office man, and thus his system fails because he does not adequately support it.

Most incompetent are those owners who are unfair to their employees. As a rule the word of a foreman or superintendent is preferred to that of a cost man; when it is a question whether to let the practical mechanic go or show up the costs accurately, the system is generally the one to suffer.

In a manufacturing town near Chicago the business manager of a concern said he could not afford to let bookkeepers interfere with the operations of the factory by discharging (as he must have done if he had put in a cost system) four or five foremen who had been with him for years and were unwilling to bother to make up reports for the cost department.

Another class of incompetent owners depend entirely upon their employees, yet are not able to criticise their work intelligently. They are just as unfair as those who make their dependents fear them. Such a course does not compel results. The fear of censure or discharge is held over the men constantly. Their confidence is never asked and of course never offered.

In planning a system, do not disregard local conditions and devise something so ideal that it cannot be applied in practice. Do not try to get accurate time records or piece work costs by depending upon ignorant workmen to fill out complicated reports, or allowing them to turn in without verification their own count of piece work. Collusion is certain; padded pay rolls and heavy costs will bring definite and unsatisfactory results. Nothing will kill a cost system so surely as this. The big question for any system to settle is how to get proper results from workmen. Time clocks and checks of divers

kinds are in use. A correct system will do much to cure
the ills that arise, but you can do just as much or more
by winning the loyal coöperation of your men.

To get good results from a cost system it is essential to
consider harmony of interests. If your superintendent
is in any way opposed to the new system, teach him the
advantage of modern methods. If he is reliable and
capable, a cost system is more valuable to him than to
any other individual, because it shows him where the
leaks are; blame goes where it belongs, and satisfactory
remedies can be applied. Your bookkeeper, too, will
welcome the knowledge that an expert can give him, for
he himself may in time become an expert, or at least
learn enough to make himself more valuable, not only
to you but also to himself. Your fellow officers, too,
must be in harmony in desiring certain results and in
being willing to pay for them.

R EPORTS *of time, materials and expense that bring
cost data to the accounting department—the books
necessary for the gathering of final results.*

Good bookkeeping, an accurate inventory and an easy
way of bringing necessary data to the cost clerks are the
basis of any cost system. Each concern differs from
every other, but as a rule the cost system should not be
allowed to interfere with the general accounting.
Especially is this true of a moderate sized plant where
constant economy is the watchword. Cost keeping and
bookkeeping in such a plant can be closely bound together, and one need not interfere with the other.

To carry on a perpetual inventory your purchasing
and receiving departments must supply the accounting
department with accurate reports of materials received.
Let the factory show an accurate account of all supplies

and materials used or on hand and the amount of labor expended on them. Your inventory ledger will then show not only the value in dollars and cents of charges and credits, but will place before you the quantities received and used. By keeping a ledger inventory and having your finger on materials all the time, you can make adjustments as required, and locate the cause of errors. The saving effected by the use of a book inventory is worth thousands of dollars to firms which spend that amount each year in weighing up material on hand.

Whether you depend entirely on a timekeeper or use time slips filled out by workmen, you must make an accurate division of all labor so that the finished product is charged as far as possible with all factory costs.

If your factory is turning out only one product, you will find it easy to add the overhead expenses to the raw material and factory charges. If you manufacture a diversity of products and various kinds of machines, then you must devise a more elaborate scheme so as to arrive at a comparison of results, and show cost by departments, machines or parts.

In your business you may find it convenient to cut down on the number of books, or add to them. Above all, use common sense and judgment, and adapt your system to your particular requirements.

To operate your system completely, you must arrive at the cost of sales and the proportion of general expenses to be borne by each process of manufacture. Some kinds of business are so simple that, if monthly results are desired, you can obtain the just proportion of fixed charges by dividing the total yearly amount by twelve. Other kinds of business are so complicated that it is necessary to follow the piece work through the factory and keep an accurate record of the production costs in each department, using the amount of direct labor as the basis for pro-rating all overhead expense. In any case the correct operation of your cost system is not a cut-and-dried proposition, but a matter of observation, judgment and constant vigilance.

The same rules apply to cost systems that hold good for other systems. If your cost keeping machinery is to prove profitable and of time and labor-saving value, it must be sufficiently elastic to meet any emergency; it must be adjustable so that its installation does not interfere with the rest of the bookkeeping routine. Give your cost system these qualities and it will save confusion and preserve the good will of your factory and office force.

THE *record of what was done last year will not produce increased dividends next year, if it is only a record and no further use is made of it. By scientific accounting the manufacturer scans the details of his business with a vision multiplied many times. He looks through the accounts as a mariner looks through his reef-finding binoculars.*

—James Logan
Chairman Executive Board, United States Envelope Company

V

KEEPING TAB ON EXPENSE

By Daniel V. Casey

WHEN I tackle a new sales problem, I turn first to my record of costs. 'Are they right?' I ask. 'Am I getting the utmost of quality, output and customer service for every dollar expended? How do my expense percentages compare with last week's, last month's, last year's?' If the answer is satisfactory--if I find no leaks, no wastes, no unnecessary frills, I know my footing is safe. The rest I can trust to salesmanship.''

Thus the owner-executive of a thrifty young business phrased his idea of the *constructive use* of costs. To him the gathering of expense items meant much more than a basis for figuring prices and computing profits. He wanted the facts for that purpose. He took care to keep track of every obscure unit of outlay—even to the weekly dollar allowed for feeding the night watchman's dog. They were all included in his selling price; for he had learned amid the wreckage of another industry that untagged expenses at their best are profits gone astray and at their worst deadly drains on business vitality.

His cost sheet was more, however, than an array of dry —and sometimes disagreeable—facts. By analyzing, tabulating, reducing results to percentages and comparing these with past performances also reduced to percentages, he turned his records into a live factor in the building of his business, not only when a sales emergency called for a test of his margin and resources, but daily in the balancing, adjusting and speeding up of his factory-and-sales machine.

By this aid he marked the slightest variation from normal—whether a slump or increase in production, in efficiency, in costs. Noting these, the causes were easily traced; the fault or extravagant practice corrected; the extra-effective method passed along to other departments where it could be applied. Comparison like this is a two-edged sword in cutting costs—lopping off the wasteful activity, trimming down the efficient one by pointing a still more economical way.

F*UNDAMENTAL rules to observe in tagging expense items and bringing them all into the cost report for proper distribution and efficient comparison.*

Getting in all the items of expense is the beginning of any good cost system. Not less essential is the second step; charge every outlay in its proper place. Merely to "play safe" you must observe three fundamental rules.

First: In your accounting treat your business with no more consideration than you show a customer—as if you had no personal interest in it yourself. Charge it with every expense incurred—not merely the principal items, the direct expenditures, but every item.

Charge for your own services, for wear and tear on machinery, for depreciation of equipment, for deterioration of raw and finished stock, for rent. Your business owes you a certain sum for these accounts. They are not direct expenditures—money actually paid out. But they are none the less actual expenses which the business must pay or you must settle out of your profits. Each of these items is an expense just as truly as the pay roll you meet or the merchandise, materials or supplies you buy.

Second: Treat every sale as you would treat a department in your business. Make it stand its share of the burden—not merely actual cost of labor and material, plus expected profit—but also its proper proportion of your running expense. Just as your total receipts must carry the burden of *all* expenses, be sure the selling price in each sale bears its exact proportion. Your cost accounting system—simple or complex—should show you what this proportion is.

Third: Prove these two operations against each other. Your ledger will show the total of profits on all sales. See that this balances with the total of profits on individual sales, analyzed by departments. If it does and if the percentage of profit is what you expected it to be, then the profit you *figured* has been actually *made*. If the totals do not balance, it is because you have failed to include all your running expenses and profits have been absorbed by the neglected items.

Tagging and keeping track of occasional expenditures is a task baffling to many executives, otherwise masterful. Contrasted with the outlay for stock, labor and the like, any one of the items seems insignificant—the price of tickets to an organization entertainment, the express or teaming charge on a belated delivery, the repairs of damage to merchandise returned by a customer, the cost of a new fixture or hand tool; the list could be extended to many pages.

All of these may be legitimate and necessary charges on the business. The trouble is they are not always charged. They do not enter into the selling price of product or merchandise. Brought together, their sum might easily represent a substantial profit for the year —but a profit actually thrown away. For the customers who benefit never know that they bought their goods for less than cost, that the seller paid for the privilege of serving them.

Nor are these lost units of outlay always small. There are hundreds of merchants and not a few manufacturers who disregard, in figuring up their costs, such important elements as rent for their real estate and adequate salaries for themselves and kinsfolk employed—both virtual gifts to an ungrateful business.

G ETTING *all expenses into the cost record requires careful attention—the small or hidden item is liable to escape a purely casual classification.*

Harder still to get into the tally are payments charged to capital accounts though rightly chargeable to running expenses. More than one enterprise makes a fine exhibit of resources until the shock of some sudden reverse brings down its house of cards. Then, under the scrutiny of a trained accountant, the bills receivable discover two or three bad accounts which could have been carried along as assets only by blind pride or reluctance to face the truth; the stock on hand dwindles in value as depreciation is impartially assessed; the new equipment listed turns out to be chiefly replacements and repairs.

The pressure is all towards self-deception or optimism in accounting. When the federal corporation tax law brought net incomes, costs and valuations into the limelight, the junior partner of an old, highly rated "quality" house risked an absolute break with his chief to force a realignment of accounts and adoption of a sound cost system. The firm would have to pay no tax, but agitation of the law had turned the young man's attention from sales to accounting and financing.

The results of a quiet inquiry alarmed him. His

senior ridiculed these—until they were analyzed and proved for him. Then he argued that the proposed changes would subtract so much from apparent resources that their credit at the bank would suffer, their standing in the trade be injured. But the younger man persisted. So the warehouses were cleared of "slow" stock—remainders of pet models on which the elder man could never be induced to accept a loss inventory at less than original cost. Process stock was treated in the same drastic fashion. An accumulation of $12,000 in uncollectible accounts was charged off the books. The allowance for depreciation of factory buildings and machinery was nearly one-third of the valuation in the last annual statement.

When the readjustments were completed, the firm's resources had shrunk by $57,000. The banks, apprised of the slashing in process and the purpose behind it, accepted the scaling down of their security and continued their loans. Suppliers of raw materials had no fault to find, since the firm voluntarily reduced the credits it required by buying on a schedule framed for immediate needs. Meantime the factory organization, shocked out of its complacency by the housecleaning, pared costs right and left, invented short cuts, discovered endless economies in time, power and materials.

To such effect, indeed, that the close of the business year, May 31st, showed an increase in the firm's surplus of $9,000 over the previous twelve-month. This, with rent, depreciation on equipment and stock and a dozen other elusive expenses deducted. Prices had not been raised; quality had been maintained. But with every outlay tagged and under observation, leaks and losses and slip-shod practice had no chance to escape detection and elimination. Several unprofitable specialties on the edge of another field were abandoned and production concentrated on the better-paying lines. Customers were given the same value as before, but the factory drain-pipe tapping the firm's resources and profits was plugged for keeps.

It is no exaggeration to call this situation typical. Supply certain conditions—the prestige of an established name, the lack of aggressive competition, the protection afforded by patents or secret processes—and it is natural for a business to slip into easy ways and measure profit and progress by volume of sales rather than by net returns in hard cash. Particularly if it be a one-man enterprise, with the owner absorbed in selling, the development of new products, or the maintenance of quality. Because costs are not a life-or-death matter—as in the business without protection other than its manager's energy and acumen—expenses are not tracked back through petty wastes, and the extravagant methods forced into line with sound practice and economy.

Twice in every three cases, also, the cost and accounting methods of the growing factory or store are the last to be adjusted to the quickened pace of the business. At the start, the manager's personal supervision of details informs him of every outgoing cent and keeps cost before him as his most important daily concern. Every expenditure is watched jealously, entered, studied with a view to lessening it or cutting it out altogether—and so he gets his cost basis down to bed-rock. When expansion comes, his assurance as to costs remains until some emergency or outside impulse undeceives him and drives home the need of a system for keeping tab on expenses to replace his former personal touch and first-hand knowledge.

In some progressive industries and trades, this impulse

has come from the general trade association. The National Association of Stove Manufacturers, for example, undertook several years ago to develop a uniform cost system. The cost sheets of several companies were analyzed and compared, the red tape cut out and only the essential elements preserved. The result was a system which suggested all the items of expense in the making of a stove and provided an easy way to record and summarize them. Tried out by various members, the composite system stood the test and was approved by the association.

Intensive analysis of the elements entering into costs is the vital thing in this model system. Every casting, rivet and washer used in construction is priced and included in the general total. Processes are segregated and, like materials and fittings, the labor and manufacturing outlay on each is put down in dollars and cents.

PERCENTAGE *division of "burden" makes each department of the business bear its proper proportion of the total of all items entering into expense.*

Expense—the elusive "overhead" or "burden" which covers a host of wastes and neglected small outlays in many businesses—is figured by percentages. It is assessed by departments and even by operations, the percentages used having been determined from test runs and past records. In the foundry, two allowances are made before the total cost of castings is computed. Finally the percentage for general foundry expense is added and the castings move on into the shops—where again they are charged with labor costs and expense percentages. In like manner provision is made for keeping track of other materials in process, including four

.grades of steel, three classes of iron and forty kinds of fittings and finishing materials.

The percentage for general manufacturing expense is not assessed until the stove is assembled, blacked and crated for shipment. Then in cumulative succession are charged loss and waste, general distributing expense, salesman's expense and finally discounts and rebates to dealers. All of these are worked out as percentages, based on past operations. Pig iron, the one factor in production subject to constant fluctuation, is set down at the arbitrary price of $16 a ton and is corrected by adding or deducting the market difference for net weight of castings.

"Average cost when paid for" is the final and most significant entry. It is the sum of all the units of expense collected above, from the pig iron in the castings and the cost of melting to the discounts and other allowances given the dealer. That this is the correct basis on which profit and selling price should be figured goes without saying. Yet in how many factories or commercial houses—outside the big organizations and a few intensely competitive fields—could the head or the sales manager tell you accurately what is the "average cost when paid for" of any article produced or sold? "Warehouse cost," four or five stations up the line, is the usual base of operations.

Like the standard system devised by the employing printers of the country, the stovemakers' effort was not directed towards the fixing of uniform prices. The printers worked out and recommended the various percentages of depreciation to be charged on machines, type and equipment, the rate to be deducted for bad debts and the profit percentage to be added to basic costs. The stove association, producing individual lines, stopped with a single recommendation, suggesting that one per cent be added to warehouse cost to take care of general factory loss and waste.

Keeping track of expenses is not an end—only a means to an end. One industrial leader gave it as his opinion recently that a cost system was good only when it showed where to use the pruning knife. It is not enough to know how to get your expense figures and to know what they are. You need to know what they should be and how to cut them, without interrupting the rhythm of production or sacrificing quality.

What, then, should a good cost system show? Here is the way a well known expert accountant summarized its purpose in an address before the national convention of box makers:

(1) Determine whether all materials purchased have been accounted for.

(2) Determine whether buying has been judicious — in prices and quality, and in amount of stock maintained, as shown by annual turnovers.

(3) By close analysis and comparison of the various items of cost—material, labor and expense —subdivided by departments, processes, or individual jobs or contracts; throw the spotlight upon the leaks and make their correction imperative.

(4) Determine the profit on different classes of work, goods or orders so that effort can be directed to the best-paying lines; also the profit in various plants, departments or sections, so that production can be concentrated where it is most profitable and the efficiency of weak departments brought up to the standard.

The head of an important wholesale house has applied this idea with remarkable success. He believes that initiative is just as necessary in handling expenditures as in selling goods, and that a manager's chief need is a plan to keep expense items continually before him in such form that they can be grouped and measured without confusion or mental strain.

To clinch his own control of expense, his classification of outlay extends to fifty-three items. Only one-fifth of one per cent of the company's expenditures gets into the "miscellaneous" category; all the rest are tagged and the percentage which each bears to sales, to total expense and to profits is tabulated for quick comparison with like records running back many years.

"Sundry expense," the catch-all account, is subdivided into twenty-eight items. These are given below to show how far the head of a house whose transactions run into many millions yearly has proved it is profitable to carry analysis of outgo:

Bags, for traveling men	Paper used in wrapping
Cleaning windows	Repairs
Dues to associations	Rubbish, including cleaning refuse
Elevators, also listed elsewhere	Safes, in safety deposit vaults
Excelsior	Smoking, covering cigars given customers and visitors
Exchange	
Laundry	
Matches	Soap
Milk, for cats in building	Specimens
Miscellaneous, including items that cannot be classified	Specimens, boxes
	Sprinkling
	Stencils
Nails	Tickets for entertainments
Newspapers	Twine
Packing materials	Water, for drinking tanks
Petty expense	Watchman service

The advantage of carrying the subdivision down to specific units of expenditure is apparent. The knowledge that your sundry expense has climbed abnormally possesses little value unless you can trace the increase to the specific items where waste has crept in and stop it.

Comparison in dollars and cents tells only part of the expense story, may even be misleading. To keep the various units at their proper levels and afford a real basis for comparison, they must be reduced to ratios founded on the productive factors in the business. Where product is uniform, it is enough to work out what each item adds to hour-cost, or cost per unit of output or sales.

CONTINUAL *watchfulness, repeated comparison, of results and prompt correction of all abuses— these are things that pave the way to bigger business.*

For the house making or handling many or varied lines, expenditures must be reduced to percentage ratios before any intelligent comparison can be made. But percentages are highly dangerous unless they represent actual figures verified by frequent tests, not mere guesses. The manager who knows that his basic costs for the past year have been forty-six per cent, his sales expense sixteen per cent, his "overhead" twenty per cent, and his losses and emergency expenses eight per cent, can be certain, of course, that his net was ten per cent. But if he attempts to apply these percentages, uncorrected, all through the coming year, he is almost certain to find his profit less than ten per cent. His volume may decrease, unanticipated losses may ensue, competition may boost selling costs or a score of contingencies change his percentages and make inroads on his net returns.

Working with embalmed ratios, too, he misses the building power which more progressive managers gain by constant pursuit, comparison and correction of expenditures. "Playing safe"—essential though it be for

the man who *does not know*—paralyzes sales and manufacturing initiative. The executive whose costs are live,
verified facts can hold prices at the level where quality,
volume and profit pull together for greatest results. Because he is certain what his goods are worth, he can meet
buyers squarely without asking or conceding odds. He
can cut if cutting becomes necessary. And at all times
he can offer customers maximum values and *make money*
for himself—the two things imperative on a business
planning for a tomorrow.

L*ACK of cost knowledge is a basic cause of an unsatisfactory inventory. Don't figure a job without having sufficient details. Guesses at values, without knowing the exact
amount of labor required, cause many losses. Few men,
also, have a proper knowledge of their general expense. This
results in many a profitless job. The lump quotation, too,
causes heavy losses. All quotations should be made on a
basis of all work required.*

—Charles J. True
President, True & True Company

PART II—FINDING AND RECORDING COSTS

My Working Rules

TO the uninitiated, business looks like a sense-less scrap; no plan or purpose to it. On the contrary, it is an unceasing campaign, with every detail worked out carefully—that is, if a man would win it must be such. There must be a well-defined and growing policy, with an emphasis on the growing. It is difficult for the business man, looking back over the years, to put his working rules into a sentence of a few words, so many essentials must be left out, but I might put mine as: Hit the Nail on the Head. That is, eliminate waste effort.

L. S. Starrett

L. S. STARRETT

President, the Starrett Manufacturing Company

VI

ASSEMBLING COSTS IN A SMALL SHOP

By A. B. Campbell, Jr.

Assistant Superintendent, Duval Planing Mill Company

ANY good factory cost system should accomplish several purposes. Some of these things, of course, under certain circumstances, are much more important than others. Among the important things it must do, are (1) to ascertain the cost per unit on each line of the factory product; (2) record the amount of time spent on each operation, or each order; (3) show the location in the plant, and the condition of work on each unfinished unit; (4) show the amount of direct and indirect labor, and for what the direct labor is used; (5) show also the amount of direct and indirect materials, and give the stage of development by departments; (6) show total output, average monthly output, busy time and idle time on each unit of output for the day, week, or month; (7) show cost per hour of operating each class of machines, and by departments; (8) show relative overhead and direct labor cost per hour or per unit in each department; and, finally, (9) show whether each operation is increasing or decreasing in cost, and, in the final analysis, whether you are making goods at a profit or loss.

To sum up the real cost of any order or unit of production, the cost system must comprehend: (1) the exact cost of material used, (2) the total amount of direct labor expended, (3) total amount of machine expense, (4) total amount of indirect labor and supplies, and (5) proportion of general expense.

Estimating costs and fixing prices at the average woodworking plant often depends more or less upon the guessing ability of some one man. In many other instances an elaborate cost system is installed, which does not furnish the basic information that has just been outlined, because if any one of the items enumerated is omitted, the cost cannot be right. The figuring of the exact cost is reasonably simple compared with the difficulty of obtaining the correct information from which to do this figuring. Put your cost system to the test and see whether it answers the nine principal requisites laid down, and comprehends the five factors of cost.

In a small factory, employing not more than one hundred men, it is comparatively simple to get reasonably accurate costs; but as the shop grows and develops into a plant employing hundreds, perhaps thousands of men, unless the cost system is based on right principles and develops along correct lines, trouble will eventually be encountered which will not only cost a great deal of money, but will also upset production.

The system here described of getting cost figures is used in a woodworking shop manufacturing a complete line of architectural woodwork, such as door and window frames, sashes, doors, stair work, columns and general builder's finish, as well as such special work as is usually done in a shop of this type. It employs less than one hundred men. The system basically consists of an order board envelope (Figure III), time ticket (Form I), and shop order (Form II).

The order board performs several functions: it is a graphic plan board upon which all orders in the shop are kept in plain sight until finished; it acts as a tracer, because alongside the order envelope are hung time ticket coupons which designate the progress of the order

MAKE MEMORANDA ON BACK			ORDER NO
ORDER NO.			DATE
NAME			CARD NO
JOB			STARTED
RECEIVED ___ WANTED ___			ARTICLES
STARTED ___ FINISHED ___			FINISHED
ARTICLES			RIPPING
			CUTTING
BENCH TIME			PLANING
MACHINE TIME			MOLDING
OTHER DIRECT LABOR			JOINTING
			STICKING
DIRECT SUPPLIES			MORTISING
MATERIALS			TENONING
			DADOING
			POCKETING
			BAND-SAWING
% OF OVERHEAD EXPENSE			SHAPING
			SANDING
			TURNING
			REPAIRING
TOTAL COST			GLUING

FIGURE III: Each unfinished order has an envelope on the order board and the time cards are hung each day near this envelope. The final card is stamped in red, showing that the order is completed

through the shop; and it acts as an automatic collector of costs on each order, as the time ticket coupons, upon completion of the job, are gathered together in the en-

velope and sent to the cost clerk. Incidentally it acts as
an incessant reminder of delayed orders. The detail of
operation of this board is apparent from Figure III.

L ABOR, *material and production reports that keep*
track of the progress on each job and gather accurate
data for the use of the cost department.

A daily time card is given to every workman each day
and the card is numbered. On this card are entered the
order numbers worked upon by him during that day,
total time expended, date and remarks. The time ticket
is composed of a number of coupons. On each coupon are
printed all possible operations which might be performed
in the shop. All the man has to do is to enter the order
number on starting a new order, the time started and
time of completing, the card number, and draw a line
through the operation performed.

On the envelope (Figure III) are entered the order
number, name of customer, the job, and the date upon
which the order was received, the date when delivery is
wanted, time the job was started and the date upon which
it was completed, together with a description of the articles, the direct labor hours spent on the job, the material required, the amount of supplies, and the per
cent of general expense.

The coupons, Figure III and Form I, as they are
torn off the daily time card, are hung on the hook
to the right of the envelope, where they are allowed to
accumulate until the job is completed, when it is designated by the word "Completed" stamped on the last
coupon. Then the total cost is figured, after which the
stubs are placed in the envelope and filed away. The
shop order (Form II) is of the ordinary type and requires
but little explanation. The rough cutters check their

work in Column "R," machine men in column "M," benchmen in column "B," and shipping clerks in column "S." This facilitates the cost work.

FORM I (front sheet): This daily time coupon is used for each job.
FORM II (back sheet): On the shop order copy rough cutters check their work in column "R," machine men in column "M," and so on

The shipping order is a copy of the shop order and needs no explanation. These five items constitute the purveyors of the figures from which the costs are computed and Figure IV illustrates the method in which they operate.

As each new job is received, it is carefully itemized and entered in the usual loose-leaf order record book. Shipping orders are made out for all stock items while shop orders are made up for such articles as must be specially manufactured. All shipping orders, as shown by Figure IV, go directly to the stock room, where they are filled from stock, thence to the shipping room, while shop orders go to the various foremen and follow on through the mill until the articles are shipped or placed in the warehouse. So far as the shop orders are concerned, no distinction is made between those for special work and those for stock work as yet. Every job is numbered and every order for that particular job is distinguished by that number followed by an initial.

For instance, an order for window frames might be marked 1749-A while an order for newels might be 1749-M. Before an order leaves the office an order envelope (Figure III) is prepared, and hung in its numerical position on the order board.

Every morning each employee is provided with a daily time card (Form I) which has been previously prepared in the office. This card is filled out as has already been explained. Each night his foreman carefully checks the card and returns it to the office. The bookkeeper now takes all the cards sent in by the various foremen, and after the total time and the order numbers shown by the coupons are copied in the proper places on the upper portion of the cards, the coupons are removed, the date stamped on each, and they are then hung opposite the corresponding envelopes on the order board. The upper portion of the card, which just fits a five-by-three-inch drawer, is filed for reference.

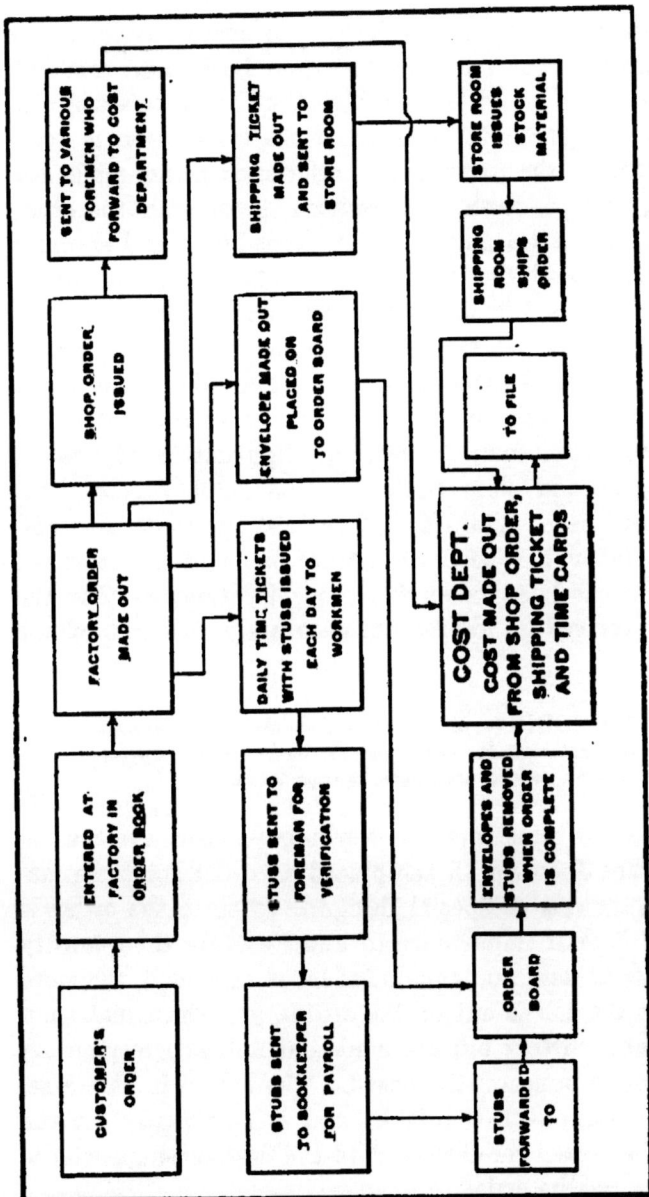

FIGURE IV: This chart shows how the order board is used to collect data for the cost department and how the important mechanical features fit into the general mill system

When an order is completed, the order envelope and coupons are removed from the order board and totals of the bench time and the machine time are entered on the envelope. The total amount of materials used is computed from the cutting bill, allowance being made for waste, and so forth, and written down with the other items. The total amount of indirect labor and supplies is entered and the portion of overhead expense which this order bears is also noted, with any other miscellaneous expense which may be charged directly to the job.

The overhead expense, which is figured on the direct labor hours basis, includes such items as indirect labor, repairs, maintenance, heating, lighting, rent, taxes, insurance and depreciation. The total factory cost has now been obtained. The cost of materials and direct labor has been accounted for, and all overhead expense has been taken into consideration, so that the figure arrived at represents accurately the cost of the job.

F INDING *the essential facts from the production data gathered by means of the order board—correct costs on each job which goes through the shop.*

To better illustrate the workings of this system, assume that John Smith has placed an order for some mahogany newels of special design, and since the order is special it is of importance to know exactly the quantity of material used and amount of labor expended, the more so that the job is out of the ordinary. The usual shop order and cutting bill are made out and a corresponding envelope is hung on the board. The order, in this case, is, for example, No. 1922-D, and is now ready for the mill. A messenger carries it to the first foreman who is to work on the order.

Along with this shop order are the necessary detail drawings. The shipping order is carried to the stock room and the necessary raw material is forwarded to the various departments. Time coupons, 1922-D, are handed in to the office each night attached to the men's time cards. The first coupons will be pink, indicating that the rough cutters have worked on the order. The next set will be blue, showing that the machine men are busy, while the yellow coupons, which follow, make known the fact that the bench men have been at work on the order and that it will soon be completed. As soon as the job is done the foreman stamps the last coupon (in this case yellow) on the time ticket of the last workman on the job, "Complete," so that when it is hung on the order board it is definitely known that the job is done. When the newels have been delivered, the envelope and coupons are removed from the board and the actual cost is determined, as explained.

There are several features of this system which are worthy of mention: in the first place, it is extremely simple; in the second place, it is known each day just what was done the day before, what operations each man performed and how long it took him to perform them, and how much it cost—and it is possible at any time to tell exactly what any job has cost up to date and how near it is to completion. By using the color scheme, it is only necessary to look at the order board and tell at a glance just what department was last to work on any one order. By comparing the date of the last coupon with the date when shipment is wanted, as shown on the envelope beside it, a back schedule order may be traced and late shipments reduced to a minimum.

The coupons, when the work on an order is completed, may be put in the envelope and filed away for future in-

formation. These envelopes will then give a definite
basis from which to estimate new or similar work. The
other advantage is that it requires little time, on the part
of the men or foreman. It greatly reduces the office
work and enables the tracing of orders through the mill,
comparison of costs, and the centering of responsibility
for mistakes. Above all, it produces the necessary figures
for determining real costs.

RECORD *making—building up a team interest in the
game—that's the basis of my method of cutting down
losses in the shop. Each department holds a definite position
in relation to the making of the product. Each takes a pride
in the work of his section. And when he sees in black and
white the results of his efforts to keep up department efficiency,
that score helps hold his interest.*

—R. B. Wilson

President, The Chicago Shipping and Receipt Book Company

VII

HOW TO FIND WHAT SMALL PARTS COST

By J. Earle Riley

IT IS possible in every business to keep accurate labor and material costs on each order going through the factory. Yet, very often a manager considers it not advisable because of the great amount of detail and expense attached to building up an accurate system which in itself not only increases that cost, but increases it to no advantage because the final cost, when once obtained, is not worth the extra money and effort.

In many kinds of manufacturing this condition is found, but in none to a greater extent than in the jewelry factory. Consequently, a description of the difficulties in such a factory has suggestions for the managers of many other kinds of manufacturing plants.

Jewelry is marketed on the basis of "what will it sell for" rather than "what did it cost." Sometimes a manufacturing jeweler handling a gold and silver line has a gross profit of one hundred or even three hundred per cent. This profit is often greater in the novelty lines. "With this fact in mind what material difference does it make," says the average manufacturer, "if one order does cost me more or less than my estimated cost ?"

Moreover, jewelry manufacture is one of those businesses in which you can estimate pretty closely, within a few cents, the material and labor cost of any line of goods when the factory is worked under normal conditions. But the place in which the jewelry manufacturer fails, is when he under-estimates his general expense. In the jewelry business, as in many other businesses where small parts are made, the items of general expense are very numerous and it often happens that at least one of these items is wrongly charged.

PECULIARITIES *which render it difficult for the manufacturer of jewelry to get accurate costs on his product—pitfalls which must be avoided.*

In manufacturing, the jeweler changes his line at least three times a year. The total number of patterns in this line may run from five hundred to two thousand or over, according to the size of his plant. Each time a line is changed a great many patterns have to be discarded and possibly ten to fifty per cent new patterns added. In adding these new patterns a tool cost must be found for each. This cost is very seldom less than ten and more often is thirty to fifty dollars.

The clever manufacturer must keep his tool cost accurately, and proportion it against his normal output so that each pattern will carry its burden. Those patterns which do not pay their own tool cost should be discarded or redesigned so that they will.

When a pattern is a "good seller" it does pay its tool cost. In a large line it is very seldom that over twenty per cent of the entire line are good sellers any one season. It is evident, therefore, that these good sellers, in addition to offsetting and carrying their own tool costs and showing a profit, must be burdened with the tool cost of the rest of the line.

Now, although it may sound strange, the majority of

jewelers are not able to tell which are their best sellers. Within the last few years two jewelers adopted a card system of individual pattern sales. They now use this system entirely in discarding and making up their lines. They found the system necessary because the salesmen disagreed as to which were the best sellers. After the card system had been running a season the men were called in and their opinion asked on the selling possi-

PRODUCTION ORDER NO	ARTICLE	DATE OF ORDER
		DATE WANTED
		DATE COMPLETED

TO

PLEASE EXECUTE THE FOLLOWING ORDER. BE CAREFUL TO ENTER THIS ORDER NUMBER ON ALL LABOR CARDS AND MATERIAL REQUISITIONS PERTAINING TO THIS ORDER. SEND THIS COPY WITH THE WORK. RETURN TO OFFICE WHEN COMPLETE

QUANTITY	DESCRIPTION	
PLANT ORDER NO	ARTICLE	DATE OF ORDER
		DATE WANTED
TO		DATE COMPLETED

PLEASE EXECUTE THE FOLLOWING ORDER. BE CAREFUL TO ENTER THIS ORDER NUMBER ON ALL LABOR CARDS AND MATERIAL REQUISITIONS PERTAINING TO THIS ORDER. RETURN THIS COPY TO WORKS OFFICE WHEN COMPLETE

ARTICLE					
DATE	MATERIAL	VALUE	DATE	MATERIAL	VALUE

LABOR	OPERATION	LABOR			HOURS	TOTALS	
		OPERATOR	QUANTITY	AMOUNT			
						MATERIAL	
						LABOR	
						EXPENSE	
						TOTAL COST	
						COST PER EMPLOYEE	

FORM I (middle card): The order for tools is made out on this card. FORM II (front card): The reverse of the first blank, this card summarizes costs. FORM III (back card): This is the production order

bilities of each pattern. The result was astounding. Patterns which they were willing to wager were great sellers, according to the cost record had not paid their tool cost, and some which each thought were poor sellers were making the profits for the business. These manufacturers now discard patterns when the records on the sale cards prove that they should do so. In every business a simple cost system has great value in this one respect of distinguishing between good and bad sellers.

The fourth pitfall in estimating small part costs in a jewelry factory is found in the details involved in getting the accurate cost of an order. Operations are short and numerous. A bench worker may have on an average, from five to nineteen orders go through his hands in an hour. To keep the cost on each order he would have to make out a time card for each. This would take him an hour and a half each day and thereby much of his production time would be lost. In a shop of one hundred men about eight thousand time cards would have to be turned out every day. It would take five or six people working at posting alone to accumulate the costs; two more would be necessary to get the results together, ready for the accountant.. Obviously no manufacturing jeweler can see his way clear to adopt a time card system.

With these four conditions, which are common to many other businesses besides the jewelry line, how can a manufacturer find the cost of what he is doing without paying too much for that privilege? Primarily costs can be estimated by obtaining costs on sample parts and letting these costs stand for all goods in that line. Material, labor and general expense are the items to be considered in getting these costs. And in the items of general expense the one of tool costs is most important.

This is the way one manufacturer has solved his cost problem. In the first place the job system of handling orders was thoroughly reconstructed. With this job system as a basis and by an accurate accounting and proportioning of general expense and by estimating labor and material costs on sample parts, this manufacturer obtains nearly all the benefits of a cost system without estimating material and labor records on each order which goes through the plant, once the sample lines have been established.

On every new pattern an accurate tool cost is obtained first of all. Orders for tools are put in the plant on Form I. This form is printed in duplicate. The orig-

EMPLOYEE NO.	DATE				STRIKING
					SOLDERING
EMPLOYEE NAME	ORDER NO.				TRIMMING
					COLORING
					POLISHING
QUANTITY	DESCRIPTION				BURNISHING
					PIN TONGUEING
					STONE SETTING

7	8	9	10	11	12	1
1	2	3	4	5	6	7

TIME	PIECE	APPROVED	HOURS	RATE	VALUE

FORM IV: *Labor costs on all jobs performed at hour rates are quickly and accurately summed up on this form*

inal is thin paper; the duplicate is cardboard. The back of the cardboard copy is arranged in columns as shown in Form II. Labor costs on this order are kept on Form IV.

In order to fill out each salesman's line at the beginning of the season a number of samples of each pattern are made. Accurate costs of both labor and material are kept on these. A production order is made out similar to that shown in Form III, the back of which is arranged like the back of the cardboard duplicate of

Form I. Labor cost is kept on sample manufacturing orders with the same sort of time card as is used in obtaining the labor on the tool costs.

Costs so obtained are collected on Form V so that after

		TIME		$	NO.
		MIN.	HRS.	PER HR.	AMOUNT
	GOLD DWT $				
	BENCH WORK				
	BENCH WORK				
	BENCH WORK				
	PRESS WORK				
	POLISHING				
	SETTING				
	LAPPING				
	COLORING				
	STAMPING				
	TOOL MAKING				
	TOTALS				
DESCRIPTION	SHOP EXPENSE				
NAME	STONE				
NO.					
DATE	GRAND TOTAL				
QUALITY	NO. OF PIECES				
PIECES MADE	COST PER PIECE				
BY WHOM MADE					

FORM V: By checking on this card every item of expense in manufacturing a sample, a cost standard is set up for that pattern

the samples have been run through the factory a cost card is available for each pattern to be used that season.

When the orders come in from customers the average quantity of any one pattern is generally about one dozen, except on the first-of-the-season order, when it is generally two of a kind. Therefore, the cost obtained on a trial lot is very close to the cost on every lot. To the labor and material cost are added the tool cost and the general expense, which are figured as percentages on every dollar of labor.

By means of the job-order system all detail is centralized so that orders can be pushed through faster, and by systematizing, production costs can be lowered.

At the beginning of each season there is a lull in the

business during which all time is devoted to getting out samples. During this period it is very easy for the men to keep accurate costs on their work. From time to time, the cost on any pattern is tested and any difference noted. These test costs do not interfere with the routine or the production to any extent.

In billing each order that leaves the factory a duplicate is made in a loose-leaf book, which becomes the sales book. This book has one column more than the bill-head. In this first column the factory cost as obtained on the pattern card against each item is carried out. At the end of each month, therefore, the amount of sales and the factory cost is known.

An accurate account of all material is kept and the factory charged with that which goes into manufacturing. It is also charged with all producing labor and general expense with the indirect labor.

In the general ledger these accounts shape as follows:

MATERIAL

DR.	CR.
Inventory.	Material put into manufacturing.
Purchases during the month.	Balance is material on hand.

LABOR

DR.	CR.
Pay Roll (from cash book).	Producing labor to manufacturing.
	Indirect labor to general expense.

This account closes each month.

Each season's tool cost is computed from time cards given in by the tool room, and the tool account is charged with the whole amount. In order to correctly apportion this cost against the season's output this account is charged off through general expense against manufacturing. As a season usually runs four months, one-fourth is charged off each month.

In this way there is either a debit or a credit balance in general expense each month. If the balance remains a small debit balance, the percentage is correct; although as this balance increases general expense gains on output. This being the case the percentage rate must be increased unless the reason for this increase is known and it is certain that it will go back to normal again. The rule works in the opposite way on the credit side where, if the credit balance is too high, too large a percentage is charged.

These accounts in the general ledger are as follows:

TOOL ACCOUNT

DR.	CR.
Season's tool cost.	Offset at one-quarter rate against four months of season so that each season's output stands its own expense.
	Posted to general expense.

GENERAL EXPENSE

DR.	CR.
Indirect labor (from labor cost).	Offset at fixed percentage to manufacturing.
Superintendence.	
Rents, insurance, taxes.	
Light, heat, power.	
Depreciations.	
Supplies.	
Maintenance and replacements.	
Incidental expenses.	
Tool cost (from tool account).	

Considerable detail is involved in carrying out this accounting but results will repay your labor. In some seasons the general expense is high, in others low. By figuring it once a year you strike an average only. As shown above, the rate is corrected each month. The moment any strange condition sets in you know it. A great amount of money is saved in this way which it is not possible to save when on January 1st you fix a rate based on the past year to apply on the coming year, in which conditions may be far different.

Most of the detail work has been performed in building up the following:

MANUFACTURING OR OPERATING ACCOUNT

DR.	CR.
Material (from material account).	Production at cost obtained from shop orders.
Labor (from labor account).	
General expense (from general expense account).	
The balance is work in process.	

PRODUCTION OR FINISHED GOODS ACCOUNT

DR.	CR.
Production at cost from manufacture.	Sales at cost from sales book.
The balance is finished goods on hand.	

SALES

DR.	CR.
Cost of sales from sales book.	Selling price of sales from sales book.

The balance equals gross profits and from this you deduct the selling expense to obtain net profits. The latter are closed into profit and loss.

There are many other general ledger accounts which go to build up such a balance sheet but they do not affect the cost accounting.

There is only one disadvantage in this method of figuring costs. The system is based on the assumption that the factory is working under conditions of normal or forced production and gives its best results under such conditions only. When business is extremely dull, the workmen know it and in order to keep themselves at work they loaf at what few jobs they get. This upsets the cost of each pattern to some extent, but not enough to affect profit.

*G*ET *daily condensed records of important statistics—it is difficult for me to understand how some manufacturing executives believe they are speaking authentically when quoting from reports compiled six months or a year ago and are content to refer to these when considering their present condition.*

This takes time, you say, and money. Yes, but the time to insure against the loss of your ship is not after it reaches mid-ocean. You may have a fighting chance when affairs reach the stage where they attract your attention; still you may not be able to find the leak in time; it may have grown so large as to be past your control.

—Edward D. Easton
President, Columbia Phonograph Company

VIII

KEEPING LABOR RECORDS BY MACHINERY

By W. B. Jadden

District Sales Manager, Felt and Tarrant Manufacturing Company

BY INSTALLING an adding and computing machine operated by a young woman, the services of three men were done away with in the estimating department of a Kansas City structural steel company. All of their time had been occupied in figuring bills, and even so they were unable to keep up with the volume of work. Not only, however, did she do all the work they had done, but it required only sixty per cent of her time. The other forty per cent she devoted to figuring material for the stock keeping department. Careful investigation of the same sort that accomplished this result brought about the installation of a machine in the timekeeping department; here also a single girl now takes the place of two clerks, and she not only does their work, but obtains results that are absolutely accurate in much less time than was required by them.

Analysis of your pay roll methods may show equally surprising results. For, no matter what the size of the plant, the general handling of the labor records is much the same, although details may differ. A profitable method of handling labor statistics in a two-thousand-man factory might be unavailable for the thumb nail records in a two-hundred-man shop. But if the managers of both factories were to list chronologically the steps in the handling of their labor records, they would not find them greatly different, one from the other.

When such an analysis is made, your opportunities for tying up loose ends and making a better system will probably be found at much the same points as were those in the factory described above.

When the labor records were analyzed in this factory, it was found that the operations in handling them could be divided into thirteen parts: (1) records of names of workmen and applicants; (2) records of total time men worked; (3) records of what men spent their time on; (4) checking of 2 and 3; (5) clerical work involved in rating; (6) clerical work involved in computing wages; (7) clerical work involved in classifying labor totals; (8) filing work; (9) making out pay roll; (10) making out pay envelopes; (11) checking envelopes with pay roll; (12) counting out money; and (13) time distribution.

LOCATING *losses in the work of finding labor cost details—substituting machines for men to save loss in the performance of routine clerical work.*

After the clerical labor situation had been analyzed in this way, the first step was to see where the greatest losses were in handling and how they could be prevented. It was found that much of the clerical work could profitably be done by machinery. Addressing machines, time clocks and records and adding machines were fitted into the routine wherever possible.

Records of workmen were first overhauled and investigated. It was found that the names could be set up, rate files printed and pay rolls printed, all on an addressing machine. The routine of this department was rearranged so that this work became the duty of the addressing machine operator. The balance of the system was changed, so that now, when a workman enters the plant, he goes first to a rack at the gate and obtains his clock card and then rings in on the clock in the department in which he works. After so doing, he places his clock card in a rack nearby. This is locked as soon as the whistle blows for commencing work; thus late arrivals, in addition to being detained at the entrance a limited time as a penalty for arriving late, are forced to go to the foreman or manager of their departments in order to get their cards in the box. When the timekeeper makes his call at the rack, if the card is not in the box, it is necessary for the foreman to explain why it is not.

A few minutes before quitting time the rack is opened to allow employees to secure their cards to ring out, and, after ringing out in the department, the workman deposits his card at the entrance. Thus is eliminated all possibility of favoritism to late or absent employees, and it is also known just how long each operative was in his department and how long he should have been producing.

The investigation was carried into the time-spent records department. Here everything was formerly done by the most tedious methods. It was found that the time-spent records could be worked up much cheaper and quicker by the use of the addressing machine. The rest of the routine was revised to conform with the installation of this machine, and is now handled as follows: the name and check number of each operative and the date of pay period is printed on each clock card by means of the addressing machine. The clock card is made with a detachable coupon at the top which bears the check number of the operator and the date of the pay period.

On the beginning of the pay period, this coupon is detached and retained by the worker to be used on pay day as his identification card; he presents this coupon and gives his name. If both check with the pay envelope, he receives his money, and the paymaster retains the coupon. The color of the clock cards is changed each pay period.

In determining what each employee did each day, and the time consumed in doing it, it was found that the work was entirely clerical, and a great deal of time could be saved by the installation of time records. The method of handling this part of the work in conjunction with time records is as follows: a time slip is filled out by a department clerk on which the following items appear: check number of the worker, date, work done and number of units finished, premium number, premium rate, basic wage rate, total points made and earnings based on a standard number of points allowed, plus a percentage of the premium points.

On the day following that on which these slips are filled out, they are checked against the clock cards for total time worked, and also against the production records. In all cases, without exception, checking on time and production is done by the labor department and never by the foreman or his assistants. Any variance in the records is immediately called to the foreman's attention and corrected at that time.

R EVISED *routine in the timekeeping and cost departments resulted in a large saving of time and clerk hire, and the number of errors was lessened.*

The time slips, after being checked for time and production, premium number and rate, are sent to the computing division to be figured and made ready for pay roll and labor cost records. From now on the work is simple mathematics and is performed, not mentally or with pencil and paper by clerks with their inaccuracies, as formerly, but at high speed with absolute accuracy on machines.

The first step in the computing division is to rate each time slip, by which is meant filling in the employee's rate per hour, whether for premium or day work. To facilitate this, the rate cards are filed consecutively according to check numbers by departments. Any change in the worker's rate per hour is promptly entered on this rate card, becoming effective only at the beginning of a new pay period.

The time slips are passed to adding and computing machines, instead of to the half dozen clerks that were formerly required to do the work. Great care was exercised in the selection of these machines and the results of their work have many times repaid the original outlay.

The adding and computing machines are then so arranged that one operator makes the detail extensions and additions while another operator checks accumulatively. By this method the checking is done with greater speed, and the work is absolutely accurate. With the former clerks, it was never known whether the results were accurate or not, and the checking was done in haphazard fashion, if done at all.

After the time slips have been figured and checked, all extensions and additions known to be absolutely accurate, the time slips are ready for the labor distribution division. Here, again, all the work was formerly done in long hand, but a careful study of the system of distribution pointed out many operations in which a machine could be used and the cost of two or three clerks saved.

A clerk places the proper signal after each labor charge. This can be done only by one well acquainted with factory conditions. After this has been done, it is the simplest of operations to collect amounts charged to the various signals by using adding and computing machines, because the operator, without removing her eyes from the time slips, adds the items she is collecting as fast as her eye can pick them out. As a check on this clerk, the aggregate sum of the various charges made during the pay period must balance with the pay roll. The percentage distribution of individual labor charges is secured accurately and easily—which is a most important consideration. These results are also obtained at much less expense and with greater rapidity by means of these machines as against the former "slipshod" method.

After the labor distribution has been secured, the time slips are filed according to check numbers, by departments, until the end of the pay period, when the total amount due each worker is computed.

The labor saving investigation was carried further in the pay roll department. The work of every clerk was analyzed, and wherever any work was found that could be economically done by machines, it was assigned to the duties of a machine operator.

The pay due each employee is next determined and checked, and entered on the pay roll sheet. As these sheets have already been run on the addressing machine, the check numbers of the men are in consecutive order and the sheets are arranged according to departments. As the time slips for each man are collected, and the bunches arranged consecutively by check numbers and by departments, it is not only an easy matter to enter on the pay roll sheet the pay due each employee, but the checking of the posting and the footing of the pay roll can easily be done on an adding and computing machine. One operator now adds the entries on the pay roll sheets by departments and the other adds the amount due as noted on the reverse side of the last time slip for the pay period for each operative in the department. These two totals must balance. The pay roll is now made up— not by mental labor, but practically all by machinery.

A change or denomination sheet is next drawn up. Here, again, mechanical devices supplant mental work. It is easily done by sliding a steel guide over the keyboard of an adding machine. This guide leaves exposed alternate keys in the machine, which is now used as a counting device. In this manner, the number of twenty, ten, five or one-dollar bills and the fifty, twenty-five, ten, five or one cent pieces required is easily computed; the speed of getting the denominations depends entirely on the ability of the operator to analyze correctly an amount into its integral parts.

How is the pay roll spent? Are the profit producing employees retained and rewarded according to their merit? Is there tangible evidence of what is transpiring in the works? Where are the leakages and what must be done to remove them? These are the questions that the investigation answered. The equipment and the methods at present in use are the mediums of answer to these questions.

A JUSTLY *discontented force can cost you more directly and indirectly than the most expert and costly supervision can ever find out.*

—William C. Redfield
Secretary of Commerce

IX

HOW TO APPORTION "OVERHEAD"

By Sterling H. Bunnell

ALL work performed by a factory organization is classified as "productive" or "non-productive." While other terms are used to define these classes, the above are fairly satisfactory in indicating the distinction between that part of the work done by the employees which, as it is sold to outsiders, is productive of income to the factory, and the other part of work, which, as it cannot be charged to any unit of manufacture, is not sold, and in a certain sense does not produce income.

The net cost of the "productive" division of the factory work consists of material and labor; this is better defined as the "prime" cost. As the non-productive work brings in no direct income, its cost must be considered a charge on the cost of the productive class, and thus there arises the conception of "gross" cost of productive work, consisting of material, labor, and the "burden" of the non-productive work.

The manner of apportioning the burden against the several orders in progress for productive work has received much study and various plans have been devised and used with success in suitable fields. One of the largest of these fields is that occupied by factories with labor-saving machinery, and the study of the actual cost of operating such machines with due regard to the future is of great importance.

The data required consists of an accurate expense account ranging over a period of several months of good average business conditions, a plan of the plant with the arrangement of the various tools and spaces for tool hands, and an inventory giving original values of the various tools and the approximate dates of their construction. Taking such a plan the investigator must mark off floor spaces about each tool sufficient to accommodate the workman and his supply of work in progress. If the shop is well arranged, the spaces not actually covered will not be very great, but just sufficient for convenient access to tools and work.

A SSIGNING *an hourly rate to each machine, which is distributed proportionately over every job using that machine, effectively apportions overhead.*

The ground plan can thus be laid off in irregular figures, each occupied by a tool and its contingent equipment. Similar spaces are laid off to provide for the various vise hands, erecting men, and so on. Each space with the equipment pertaining to it is a "productive unit."

It is fair to assume that the monthly expense due to the building and real estate should be paid on a basis of square feet of ground occupied. This general rule may be modified so as to assign to spaces next side walls, if much better lighted than the interior of the building, a larger share of the building expense; while central floor space two stories in height (as in a gallery shop), or spaces having crane service, should be rated higher.

The inventory of equipment is next used to set a value on each "productive unit," whether consisting of a machine and its equipment, a vise and the accompanying files, chisels and other shop tools, or a mere space on the floor where an assembler may work; in all these cases the unit is considered as lying within a definite area of floor space.

In the estimated value of a machine tool, the cost of its foundation if any, of transportation to the works and erection in position, and of countershafts and belting with all other attachments belonging exclusively to this tool, should be included. The tool and equipment must earn interest on its total value, and must also lay up a sufficient amount to replace itself at the end of its natural or probable life.

A table is now made in which appears the serial number of each tool in the shop, the name of the tool and, in columns following, the value of tool equipment, and the percentage determined upon for interest and depreciation. The amount to be earned and set aside each month for interest and depreciation is computed and set down in the next column. In making this table, the power house equipment is grouped and its interest and depreciation computed in the same way. Next comes the estimated average monthly outlay for repairs, and the monthly expense for the floor space occupied by each tool or other productive unit of space. The proportion of the monthly expense for small tools and supplies which can be readily assigned to the machines direct, as drills purchased for use in drill presses, is next estimated and set down.

The cost of operating the power plant and of lighting and heating the building is next in order. This is obtained by first computing the cost of operating the power plant, including space charge, interest and depreciation, fuel and labor cost; then estimating the average horse-

METHODS OF CHARGING "OVERHEAD"

1 DIRECT MATERIAL
A. FIND WHAT PER CENT OF TOTAL DIRECT MATERIAL ENTERS INTO EVERY PRODUCT
B. IF A PRODUCT CONSUMES .01 OF MATERIAL, CHARGE IT WITH .01 OF "OVERHEAD"
C. USE WHERE THE ENTIRE PRODUCT IS ESSENTIALLY THE SAME.

2 PERCENTAGE ON WAGES
A. FIND WHAT PER CENT OF TOTAL DIRECT WAGES ENTERS INTO EVERY PRODUCT
B. IF A PRODUCT CONSUMES .01 OF WAGES, CHARGE IT WITH .01 OF "OVERHEAD."
C. USE WHERE WAGES ARE AN IMPORTANT PART OF COSTS AND VARY GREATLY.

3 DIRECT LABOR
A. FIND WHAT PER CENT OF TOTAL DIRECT LABOR HOURS ENTERS INTO EVERY PRODUCT
B. IF A PRODUCT CONSUMES .01 OF DIRECT LABOR HOURS, CHARGE IT WITH .01 OF "OVERHEAD."
C. USE WHEN ALL WAGES ARE NEARLY UNIFORM.

4 MACHINE RATE
A. FIND WHAT EXPENSE EACH MACHINE IS RESPONSIBLE FOR; DIVIDE THIS INTO AN HOURLY RATE.
B. IF A JOB USES FOR FIVE HOURS A MACHINE RATED AT $0.10, CHARGE THE JOB $0.50 FOR "OVERHEAD."
C. USE WHERE BULK OF INVESTMENT IS IN MACHINES, AND LABOR COSTS ARE RELATIVELY IMPORTANT

5 SUPPLEMENTARY RATE
A. DETERMINE AND USE MACHINE RATE AS IN 4 SUBTRACT TOTAL "OVERHEAD" CHARGED TO SPECIFIC JOBS FROM TOTAL ACTUAL "OVERHEAD." DIVIDE REMAINDER, WHICH IS CAUSED BY IDLE TIME, INTO A "SUPPLEMENTARY RATE."
B. IF "SUPPLEMENTARY RATE" FOR ONE MACHINE IN MARCH IS $0.02, AND A PRODUCT USES THAT MACHINE FIVE HOURS, ADD $0.10 TO THE AMOUNT ALREADY CHARGED BY MACHINE RATE.
C. USE FOR 4 WHEN IDLE TIME IS IMPORTANT.

6 "COST NUMBERS"
A. DETERMINE MACHINE RATE AS IN 4 CONSIDER THIS FOR EACH MACHINE A "COST NUMBER"; IF A MACHINE RATE IS $0.75, ITS "COST NUMBER" IS 75.
B. IF ON THIS MACHINE (COST NO. 75) A JOB TAKES SIX HOURS, WHILE TOTAL COST NUMBER HOURS FOR MONTH ARE 10,000 AND TOTAL OVERHEAD IS $20,000 CHARGE JOB 6X $0.75X20/10.
C. ALTERNATIVE FOR 5.

7 INSPECTION
A. CAREFULLY INSPECT YOUR PRODUCT AND DIVIDE INTO CLASSES OF ARTICLES ACCORDING TO AMOUNT OF DIRECT COST WHICH EACH SORT INCURS.
B. JUDGE WHAT PART OF OVERHEAD EACH CLASS OF PRODUCT REQUIRES AND CHARGE ACCORDINGLY.
C. SPECIALLY SUITED TO CHARGING ADMINISTRATIVE AND SELLING COSTS.

8 MATERIAL AND PERCENTAGE ON WAGES
A. FIND WHAT PER CENT OF BOTH TOTAL DIRECT MATERIAL AND TOTAL DIRECT WAGES ENTER INTO EVERY PRODUCT
B. IF A PRODUCT CONSUMES .01 OF MATERIAL AND .02 OF WAGES, CHARGE IT WITH ½ (.01 + .02) OF "OVERHEAD"
C. USE WHERE MATERIAL AND WAGES ARE EQUALLY IMPORTANT FACTORS IN COST.

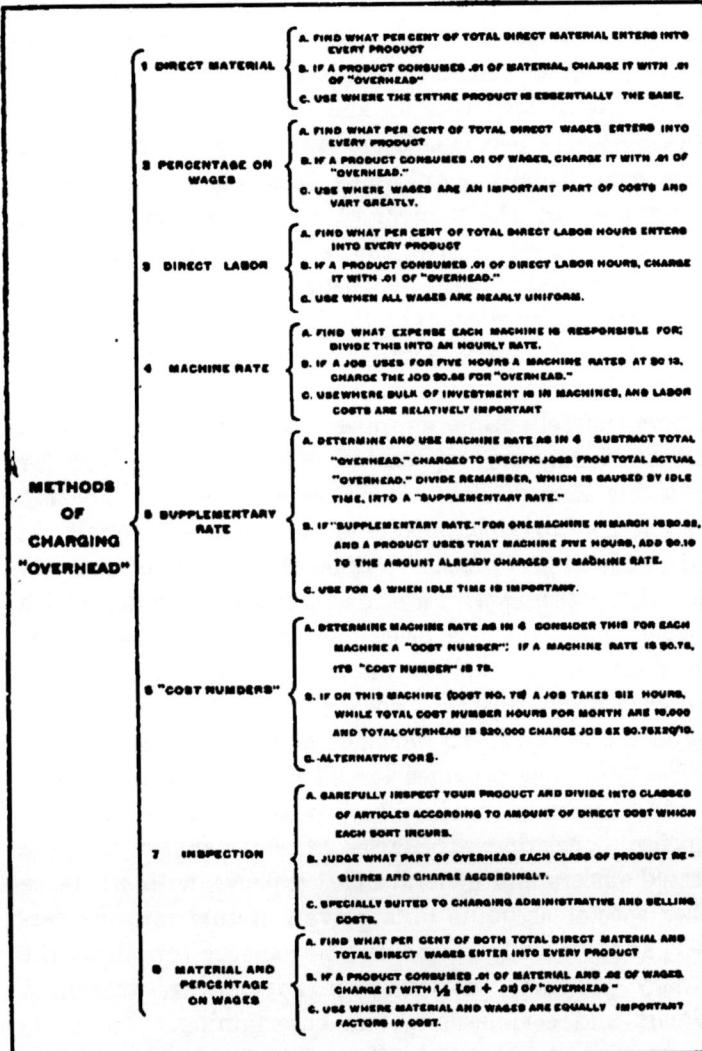

FIGURE V: These are the standard methods of charging "overhead." The aim in every case is to make each job or piece of work bear its due proportions of general expense

power required by each machine when running under average conditions. The probable running hours per month for each productive unit is next estimated; this, in the case of vise workers and floor hands, is the total working hours per month multiplied by the number of such men usually employed. Multiplying the horse-power used by the number of hours for each machine, and adding these figures, the total of horsepower hours may be compared with the usual output of the power plant, and the co-efficient of the load then determined.

The item of general shop expense remains, comprising expense for small tools not already apportioned, labor of helpers, miscellaneous supplies, loss by defective work and accidents, and expense of office work required for managing shop affairs. This item reduced·to a monthly basis seems fairly chargeable to each employee equally as it depends in great measure upon the number of men employed, increasing with a large force and decreasing with a small one. On this basis, therefore, the monthly expense may be divided by the number of men employed, and each productive unit charged with the share belonging to the workman or workmen attached to the unit.

The table now provides for all the expense which pertains to the shop itself. There is also an administrative expense, consisting of salaries of the manager and the elected officers and general office expense, with whatever other special accounts of a private nature may be carried; and generally a considerable expense for selling the factory product, consisting of advertising, traveling, salaries and commissions, and entertaining. These expenses are not connected with construction, but with administration; and are best provided for as percentages on the gross cost of the goods produced by the shop, rather than by inclusion in the table of shop expense.

Carrying across the totals for each productive unit, the total monthly expense of each is obtained; and dividing these amounts by the hours of work per month opposite, the hourly rate which should be charged for each productive unit is shown. While no two units may figure out to have the same rates, it will be found that the rates can be grouped into two, three, or more classes in which the figures fall more or less closely together. Flat rates in round numbers may be assigned to each of these groups, and substituted for the exact rates, forming a set of two or three burden rates for the whole shop.

It may be found that the rates already charged for work agree closely with the figures based on the table of correct burden charges, the calculated rates agreeing closely with unaided judgment. If, however, local customs require rates too low, the fact must be faced and altered, or disaster will overtake the business. It is seldom that the combined judgment of practical men is at fault, but variations from average conditions may bring about a state of affairs where judgment based on general knowledge only fails to appreciate that unusual action is necessary to avoid loss.

THE *system of management is but the tool of the manager Alone it is useless, may even be dangerous; the management without it is handicapped, whereas the system backed by an active mind continuously using it, is the effective combination. And labor saving management is a system that forces the executives to manage.*

—F. G. Coburn
Assistant Naval Constructor, U. S. N

X

DESIGNING YOUR COST FORMS

By S. B. Rogers,
Production Manager, Sangamo Electric Co.

A CLERK in the purchasing department of a northern brass factory ordered a five years' supply of time cards. By so doing, he thought he was saving considerable money for the company, and he did in first cost. But he neglected to figure what this purchase meant in final cost. Whether or not the form was being used efficiently was not considered. Whether or not it was of the best design for the purpose for which it was intended was not thought of. In fact, at the time the order was placed, the production department was planning to supplant this form as soon as the supply of old forms had been exhausted. The purchase clerk, not reckoning with this contingency and thinking only of an efficient purchase, went ahead blindly.

Now, if it had been the practice in this concern, as it is in all carefully managed factories, to buy no forms, old ones or much less new ones, without subjecting them to an analysis similar to the accompanying chart, this unwise purchase would have been avoided and money saved. Order your supplies of forms as judiciously as supplies of materials and new equipment.

Perhaps the first and most important item to consider is the use to which the form will be put—how, where and when it will be used, and by whom. A form used in the drafting room should embody different features from one employed in the machine shop, and a card used by the erection gang out in the yard, where it is exposed to the weather, should have characteristics that are different from one required in the wood shop. Again, if the form is to be used where there is a great deal of grease and dirt, design it for that purpose. In the pattern room the requirements are not so severe and hence a less durable form may serve the purpose just as satisfactorily.

Then, there is the question of how a form will be used —will your man fill it in with pen, pencil, or a punch, and will this information be filled in at the office or out in the shop. The design must embody a consideration of the use of a rubber stamp, a time clock, automatic recording devices and so on. Carefully consider the amount of clerical work and also the personnel of the clerks who will perform this work. In fact, all possible uses to which a form will be put must be carefully analyzed before the second step, permanency, is considered.

M ETHOD *of using a form determines the kind of card adopted—need for preservation and rough treat ment in the shop are important considerations.*

In this connection, will the form be referred to constantly? Must it be preserved for a number of years, or can it be destroyed as soon as it has been used? How many hands must it pass through? This is a vital point. To prove it, call to memory some filed-away form which, when you pulled it out, was so torn and worn that it was impossible to decipher the information on it. Other things being equal, if the form is to be used only for a limited length of time and then destroyed, there is no necessity for a thick, heavy card with lasting qualities on which the information is filled in with ink.

Again, what service must the card perform? The analysis of this question will influence the character of the form considerably. Will the information on it be used in several different departments or will it be confined to one department only? In either case, these facts must be considered in its make-up. Also, is the information on the form to be taken from other forms, is the card self-contained, or is the information collected on this form to be used in conjunction with other forms?

All of these facts determine the quality and thickness of the paper that will be required. The question of color is another vital point. Is it necessary that a color scheme be used? Often it is, and in such a case, a definite color scheme must be worked out. Know commercial weights and sizes before you attempt to design a form economically. Then again, how must the form be put up? Oftentimes it is necessary to have it perforated. This fact may alter some of the other features that have been considered. Again, if you order thick, heavy cards, they may in the aggregate be too bulky to handle and, on the other hand, if too thin and pliable, difficulty may be encountered in properly filling them out.

A great many forms require duplicates, and in order that clear copies may be obtained, it is often necessary to sacrifice weight and thickness in order to obtain these clear copies. The color, size, weight, kind of paper and number of duplicates are often the result of a compromise between various limiting conditions. Yet, within all these limits, there is a one best form under the circumstances, and it is this one best form that you should strive for, because by its use large savings may be obtained. This has been thoroughly proved by the many factories that have considered these points in designing and coordinating their various factory forms.

A Chicago factory was in the habit of using a very poor grade of paper for production orders. Oftentimes the form, before it had served its purpose, had to be

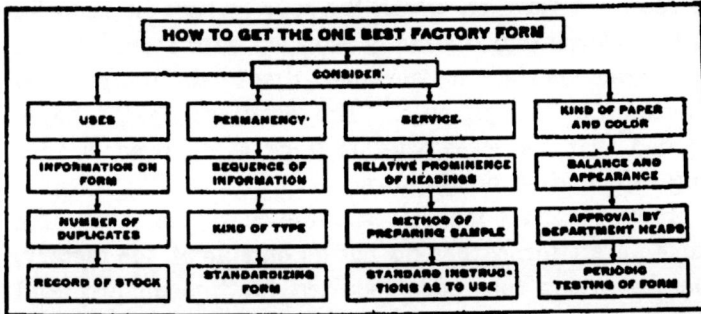

FIGURE VI: *Forms need to be tested before they are used. This chart shows the vital points to be considered in making up the design and deciding on the kind of card to use*

entirely rewritten. This fact came to the management's attention and in trying to remedy this condition, they swung clear to the other extreme. The very best and heaviest kind of paper was ordered to replace the old grade. Six duplicates of the production order were required and the new paper was so thick and heavy that it was difficult to obtain a clear sixth copy. The department which received this last duplicate complained. The result was a compromise between durability and clearness and also an investigation to find a kind of paper that would prove still more satisfactory. It is evident that all this trouble could have been avoided by a thorough consideration of the subject in the beginning.

After you have decided on the kind of paper, the next important consideration is the information that is to go on the form, and this information will determine, to a great extent, the design of the card. If possible, it should be made to conform with standard sizes, but not at a sacrifice of clearness. You should carefully look into the proper width and spacing of lines and columns. Nothing is more aggravating to a clerk or workman than to receive a form on which the space where he is to fill in his information is already crowded with facts filled in by a previous clerk or workman, due to the limited area allotted for the purpose. The headings should be so worded that the least possible work is required in putting information on the form.

Many factories make it a practice to omit the firm name on all forms that do not go outside of the factory, thereby saving the space required for this purpose and also the work of printing the name. Draw up a list of all the possible information that may be required. Then determine the relative prominence and importance of the various items and make an endeavor to eliminate all information not absolutely essential to the efficient use of the form. Superfluous data is always expensive. It attracts the attention of every one who uses the form, and the time thus consumed is evidently wasted.

L OGICAL *arrangement of information according to the order in which it is gathered in the shop or used in the cost office makes an efficient form.*

Study also the sequence of operation, endeavoring to arrange the headings and columns in the order in which they will be placed on the form. One factory, for instance, found it necessary to copy to a form for permanent record several important points from bills of lading. The form was first designed for neatness of arrangement and looks and with no regard for sequence of operations.

The design was changed so that the items were in their correct sequence—in this case, the items started in the upper left-hand corner and ran directly across the form and then down one space and back across the form and down the next space, and so on, until the work was complete.

After you have decided upon the sequence of information, the next question of importance is the relative prominence of the various headings. Which shall be placed in large, bold print and which may be reduced to small, modest type? This will depend upon several things, such as, which item is referred to the largest number of times, which is the most important for future use, which items will be copied to other forms later, and so on. Then consider such points as the intelligence of the clerks and workmen who use the forms. If they are a non-intelligent class, it is sometimes worth while to play up the item or heading that they must refer to in order that they may become familiar with its prominence rather than its actual wording, and habit will soon automatically guide the workman's pencil to the proper heading simply because it is conspicuous.

Consider your forms also in the light of balance and general appearance. Unless conditions actually demand otherwise, it is often possible to give the form this essential quality of balance. When lines and columns are used, limit them to those that are absolutely necessary. The fewer the better. In a great many cases the columns and spaces should be numbered, as this is of considerable aid when referring to the information on a form in a typewritten report or memorandum. In such a case it is only necessary to refer to a certain figure mentioned in column 2, line 4 of report, and so on.

All of the points so far discussed should now be drawn

up on a sample form. This may be done on an ordinary sheet of paper in pencil or on a sample of the paper which will ultimately be selected. The type may be set, printed on ordinary paper and pasted on this form, so that you can get a clear idea of its appearance, or you may fill in headings with ink or pencil.

Issue standard instructions explaining in clear, civil English just how these forms should be ordered, distributed, used, collected, filed and kept track of. Also endeavor to collect the common features of all forms and standardize this information. Analyze the uncommon or unlike characteristics and make an effort to standardize these. That the results of such studies will be well worth your while has been proved by all factories that have systematically carried out these methods of standardization.

R ECORDS *before every man from manager to bobbin boy key up the whole mill. They create a sympathetic hustle from the top down and from the bottom up. I keep all—overseers and second hands alike—interested by showing them how they can do better. Progressive totals of last week and today, showing how wastes and seconds are decreasing, will develop a spirit in the whole mill.*

—Henry D. Martin
General Superintendent, The I. E. Palmer Co.

PART III—COST SYSTEMS THAT PROVED EFFECTIVE

How Cost Records Guide

COST records should be made not only for the purposes of determining prices and securing efficiency, but also with the objects of discovering opportunities for economy and openings for expansion. It is not enough to know how much a job costs. It is most essential that we know *why* it costs as much as it does and the effects of this cost.

If the next job costs more or less than it did the last time it was made, the records should enable the portion of the work in which the difference exists to be promptly and accurately discovered. Indeed, this is the fundamental principle of a really truthful system of cost keeping.

The successful business of today in any line of endeavor has been built by men who have accurate knowledge of their affairs secured from keeping true records of their experiences and using them in guiding the business to a profitable showing.

A. M. GLOSSBRENNER

President and General Manager, Levy Brothers and Company

XI

HOW TO GET OFFICE COSTS

By Marshall D. Wilber
President, Wilber Mercantile Agency

SYSTEMS for computing production costs have been
adopted in the last decade by all up-to-date factory
superintendents and managers who have supervision over
"productive" work—that is, work employed in contrib-
uting to the transformation of raw material into a finished article to be put on sale on the market.

But these methods have been applied very little to the
determination of the actual costs of office work. In determining productive costs, the cost of the office work
connected with the production and sale of the article is
generally represented by a percentage computed in a
more or less arbitrary and inaccurate manner.

In some lines of business almost all cost is represented
by office labor and office expenses. It follows that any
determination of the cost of a specific piece of work
turned out, or business operation performed by such a
concern, must be procured by determining the cost of
the office labor involved. The necessity and value of cost
systems in the office is nearly if not quite as great as
in the factory itself.

An accurate system of office costs requires that each
item of expense be assigned to the proper department
and men, and compared with the figures for the same
work during other periods as far as possible; also, the

income from each employee should be noted, for an increase in cost is justifiable if a greater percentage of increase in income results. The first thing to learn is precisely what the individual working units of the company are costing and producing—clerks, stenographers and bookkeepers. When you know that, mere addition will tell you what each department is costing in and of itself. Then a careful analysis will show just what proportion of the general expense each employee should bear.

On the other hand, you can easily credit income to the department and the individual producing it. A comparison of expenses and income, with due consideration of all conditions surrounding both, will always tell just what each department and individual is doing, what profit or loss each is showing.

Suppose one mail clerk is getting five dollars a week and another six. How are you to know beyond doubt whether the second one is doing twenty per cent more work than the first, unless you possess exact records of the number of pieces of work which each of them turns out?

S TENOGRAPHIC *costs may be accurately determined by keeping time records, production data and expense statistics on every operator and each machine.*

It is comparatively simple to obtain cost records of stenographic work. Have your office manager keep a series of work sheets (Form I), on which the name of every stenographer in the office is entered, with her weekly salary opposite. Each night she reports the number of letters she has written, or the mail clerk may check the number as the work is turned in to him, by means of her initials on each letter. These figures are

WEEK ENDING										
NAME OF STENOGRAPHER	SALARY	MON.	TUE.	WED.	THU.	FRI.	SAT.	TOTAL	AVERAGE PER DAY	AVERAGE PER DOLLAR
Mary Truax	10.00	60	64	68	66	60	62	380	63 1/3	38
Anna Brown	9.00	54	56	54	58	52	50	324	54	36
Sarah Howe	9.00	52	54	50	52	56	54	318	53	35 1/3
Ella Burt	12.00	70	72	74	70	68	72	436	72 2/3	36 1/3
Maggie Thomas	8.00	50	48	46	52	50	48	294	49	36 3/4
Carrie Meyer	8.00	52	52	48	48	50	52	302	50 1/3	37 2/3
Jennie Lowe	10.00	64	60	66	68	64	58	380	63 1/3	38
TOTAL	66.00	402	386	406	414	400	396	2434	405 2/3	37
AVERAGE PER DAY	9.43	57 2/7	55 1/7	58	59 1/7	57 1/7	56 4/7	347 5/7	58 1/2	—

FORM I: This cost sheet is kept by the office manager. It shows the total cost of stenographic work, and the "average per dollar" column gives the relative efficiency of different operators entered on the work sheet. When you keep a daily individual work sheet the figures can be transferred directly from that to the cost sheet.

Thus, at the end of each week, by adding the horizontal columns, you know exactly the number of letters written by each stenographer during the week. Adding the perpendicular columns, you can learn from the first column the week's expenses for stenographic labor, from the succeeding six columns the daily number of letters written, and from the final column the total number of letters written by all girls during the course of the week.

By dividing the total expenses of stenographic labor by the total number of letters written, you get the average cost of a letter. Compare these figures with the number of letters written and the salary received by each stenographer and you know at once whether she has written above or below the average number.

Keep these records accurately month after month, and the results will show you what you are paying, on the average, for the writing of a letter. You thus have a standard, below which you cannot economically allow your stenographers to fall. Any who go above the average for a considerable period of time may be rewarded accordingly. The system thus has the double virtue of giving you the exact cost of each operation and of working perfect justice among the employees.

The work done by each kind of typewriter machine and the cost of keeping it in order may well be recorded in the same manner. For these records the office manager has the same kind of cost sheet and the machines are listed according to their numbers. Each stenographer in reporting the numbers of letters written, also reports the number of her machine. Whenever a new ribbon is called for or any repairs are done upon her machine, the number of the machine and the amount of expense are recorded. An average cost is struck from records covering a long period of time. This indicates exactly what machines are doing the best work and what machines require the greatest expense for up-keep. Such records will soon bring to light the kind of machines most economical for your use.

APPLICATION *of the cost principle to all departments of the office keeps a strict tab on the results from pay roll and incidental expenditures.*

Similar methods of keeping costs may be advantageously applied to other routine work in the office in order to ascertain the number of documents handled by billing clerks, the number of papers filed by filing clerks; even the work of the bookkeepers themselves may be recorded in such a way as to indicate the number of postings each man makes, or the time he consumes in making journal entries or taking trial balances. The slow men are inevitably singled out, and the fast workers stand in a class by themselves and receive the rewards due them.

The system does not demand an office reorganization. Records are made in the ordinary routine of the day's work at the point where they can be made most easily and quickly, and weekly summaries bring final results to a focus at your desk.

In offices where the cost system has received careful trial, its application has gone even further. The work of sub-executives is recorded in the same way as the routine motions of clerks and typists. Record of the daily number of letters dictated by correspondents, the number of calls made by outside men, and so on, through all the grades of producers, up to department managers whose business is to oversee and plan, and not to do specific things, give you a hold on office work which enables you to see the leaks at a single glance and economize in places' where haphazard management would recognize nothing out of the way.

These examples have taken account of only two items of expense: pay roll, equipment—and a small portion of supplies. In addition to all such costs, there are a large number of items still uncharged—that is, charged not to any one department or job, but to fixed expense, one of the most vague and dangerous terms in business. These weekly cost reports on individuals, when added up, tell the story of the direct expense in each department, but they tell only half the truth, and are therefore all the more likely to be deceiving. The department which shows a comparatively small direct expense may be responsible for a large part of the fixed expense; it may occupy large office space and so be answerable for a large percentage of the rent, or the work done in it may require a large amount of bookkeeping and so have a heavy accounting expense chargeable against it.

For instance, in an office occupying 6,000 square feet of space, the rent may be $200 a month. Department A in that office is occupying 1,500 square feet every month; therefore department A must be charged with $50 rent—one-quarter of the total—and the other departments with their just proportion. The same principle holds good for every item that is classed under fixed expense, from taxes to ice water. All supplies—like stationery, ink, or pens—can be charged directly to the department using them. In order to keep track of these items, supplies must be taken from the stock room only on an order showing to what department they are to go and for what purpose they will be used.

Finally, each department in your office must be charged with a due proportion of the expense of those departments which are not producing—like the administrative, for instance, the bookkeeping, or the legal. Let each productive department bear this burden in proportion to the amount of work each requires from the non-productive, or in proportion to its volume of business.

Having arrived in this way at the total expense for each department or each official, compare the present expense with that of past periods, and with the amount earned in each case, or the amount of work turned out. If the output or earning capacity has increased at a greater rate than the expense, you have a net gain, even though the actual cost figures are higher than before.

STEAM *and electricity have made possible the development of the world and these forces have made the great machinery age in which we are now living. Everything is being done on a larger scale, but there never was a time when the smallest details of a business had to be watched so closely as at present. The great problem which now confronts men in industry and commerce, and also in educational, religious and philanthropic work, is one of management and administration.*

—James Logan
Chairman Executive Board, United States Envelope Company

XII

FINDING THE COST TO SELL

By Percival Richards

UNINTENTIONALLY, goods are sometimes sold at a loss. The price maker adds a fair gross profit to the cost of manufacturing, and net profits are blindly expected to come from this difference between cost and selling price; whereas, actually, total selling costs vary almost as greatly as manufacturing costs—in fact, the ratio of selling cost often varies inversely to the cost of manufacturing.

It is essential, therefore, to figure selling costs as accurately as manufacturing costs. Otherwise you may lose valuable time and energy in selling lines of goods which do not show an adequate profit; no-profit lines may be pushed by your more careless salesmen, in order to make a good showing, where high class goods should be sold; selling expenses on particular goods may be excessive when you consider the volume of trade done.

In the average business the cost of selling may be divided broadly into:

1. Traveling salesmen.
2. Agencies.
3. House orders.
4. Overhead expense.

It is important that each of these selling costs be kept separate and up-to-date.

Each day, as orders come in from the salesmen, clerks
in your office should work out the invoice amounts and
insert selling costs at the same time in order to obtain
the total selling price and the total cost price of each
customer's entire order. Copies of orders go to the departments concerned and the original order sheets are
retained in the office and filed in numerical order, a separate file being kept for each salesman. The results thus
obtained are entered on the salesman's weekly record
(Form I).

This card places on record a summary of all orders
obtained during the week, shows the invoice values, total
cost of selling the goods, and a list of new accounts
opened. The salesman's salary and expenses and a record of percentages are entered on the back of the card
(Form II). Figures for the last corresponding trip are
also entered for the purpose of comparisons and a
monthly summary goes to the summary card (Form III),
which, when completed, gives the annual totals.

Figures for the previous year are also entered month
by month. For convenience in comparisons they are inserted in red ink above the current figures. It is well
also to total the figures in pencil from month to month,
so that the results obtained by a salesman for any period
of the year are instantly available, together with the
cost of obtaining the orders and the percentage of gross
profit and expenses. Particulars in regard to agencies
have somewhat similar records, the column for expenses
including the agent's commission.

House orders or sales made at headquarters to visit-
ing customers are recorded under the headings of the
different house salesmen. A separate card (Form IV.)
keeps the record for each individual salesman.

Here again, figures inserted in red ink show the record

of the corresponding period for the previous year, and a
summary of the monthly figures on the salesmen's cards
presents the total house sales in each department month

SALESMAN'S WEEKLY RECORD

NAME	GROUND

WEEK ENDING

CUSTOMERS' NAMES AND TOWNS	TOTAL VALUE OF ORDER		TOTAL COST OF SELLING	
STOCK LINES				
SPECIAL LINES				
TOTALS				
PARTICULARS OF NEW ACCOUNTS OPENED				

FORM I: *This weekly record is kept for every salesman, and shows the
net results of his work*

by month. Other necessary details which are shown on
the cards of traveling salesmen and agents are repeated
on the house sales card. The totals of department selling

expenses for the month complete the record on the monthly sales card.

Probably the most common error in arriving at the complete selling cost is failure properly to figure in all

SALESMAN'S WEEKLY RECORD

NAME		WEEK ENDING	
JOURNEY		DATE OF LAST JOURNEY ON SAME GROUND	
TOTAL SALES		COST OF GOODS SOLD	
GOODS RETURNED DURING WEEK		COST OF GOODS RETURNED	
NET SALES		NET COST	
GROSS PROFIT $		EXPENSES $	
PERCENTAGE OF GROSS PROFIT ON NET SALES }		SALARY $ _____	
		TOTAL $ _____	
		PERCENTAGE OF EXPENSES ON SALES }	

CORRESPONDING FIGURES FOR LAST JOURNEY ON SAME GROUND

FORM II: Printed on the reverse of Form I, this sheet is used to record percentages and comparative figures, and becomes a permanent record

overhead selling expense. This includes not only the sales manager's salary and expense and the cost of his immediate office force, but also the rental on the office space he uses, the clerical cost of maintaining records of the sales department, and so on. This total overhead expense, which does not vary greatly from month to month, is apportioned against each salesman and each

TRAVELER'S NAME_____							
1911	NET SALES	COST	GROSS PROFIT	G. P. %	SALARY, COMMISSION ETC.	EXP. %	LOCAL ADVERTISING
JANUARY							
FEBRUARY							

HOUSE ORDERS

SALESMAN_____

	NET SALES	COST	GROSS PROFIT	G. P. %	SALARY, COMMISSION ETC.	%	REMARKS
JANUARY							
FEBRUARY							
MARCH							
APRIL							
MAY							
JUNE							
JULY							
AUGUST							
SEPTEMBER							
OCTOBER							
NOVEMBER							
DECEMBER							
TOTALS							

FORM III (upper sheet): This summary card shows the annual totals, with percentage results of one salesman. FORM IV (lower sheet): Sales made at headquarters are recorded for each salesman on this card

department according to the amount of total sales. For instance, if total sales in all departments for the month are $100,000 and the total overhead expense is $1,000, then 1 per cent of the total invoice of sales in each department and for each salesman is added to the direct selling cost for indirect expense. If sales in one department or for one salesman should equal $10,000 for the month, $100 represents the indirect selling cost charged

against him. Failure to figure all overhead expenses
and distribute them properly will sometimes explain an
otherwise unaccountable dwindling in your profits, a
leak all the more dangerous because it is hard to locate.

Total sales and selling costs arranged by departments
and by individual salesmen and agents, with figures for
the corresponding period of the previous year above the
current figures in red ink, show you at a glance the total
increases and decreases, keep you into the closest possible
touch with the profit-bringing quality of your sales
department and place in your hands the key which
closes the door on slip-shod methods and weak selling
campaigns. You have valuable data on which to base
future policies, cutting out unprofitable lines and reducing sales costs to the minimum.

IN ORDER *to increase production a manager does not
study his plant in a lump sum, but goes through his shop
and analyzes each operation and movement. It often happens
that he discovers astonishing possibilities that have hidden
themselves for years in the most transparent disguises.*

—F. C. Cutler

Sales Manager, Worcester Pressed Steel Company

XIII

PLANNING A RETAIL STORE EXPENSE SHEET

By E. J. Bliss
President, Regal Shoe Company

NOT long ago a department store in the Southwest, after years of apparently profitable business, closed its doors in the middle of a busy season. The store's strong point had been its stocks. Its advertising slogan was "Everything New While It's New." It maintained standing orders for novelties with New York and Chicago jobbers. Hardly a day passed that something absolutely new was not shown in its store windows.

City stores find that not more than 70 per cent of their merchandise moves at regular prices. Seventy-five per cent would be an outside figure. The balance is sold at price concessions ranging from 25 per cent off to perhaps 20 per cent below cost. It is a fundamental principle of modern merchandising that no goods shall be carried over from one season to another. Recognized staples are possibly excepted, though in some houses even these are sacrificed. Such radical reductions representing a loss in every sale, must be balanced; otherwise a store will find itself upon the rocks in short order.

This was what undermined the southwestern store. Its volume was large enough. The ratio of sales to purchases was not disproportionate. But doing a novelty business, it did not get enough for its goods. Its owners entirely neglected to figure that their frequent price reductions, necessary to move odds and ends or slow lines, amounted to considerable sums which, not taken care of in the overhead charges or selling expense, quickly absorbed the profits.

Through this failure to provide for normal depreciation of stocks and necessary price reductions toward the end of the regular seasons, many merchants have come to grief. Mercantile agencies report that a large percentage of retail failures are directly due to the owner's belief that a business is making a profit, when, as a matter of fact, it is running at a loss. The only way to be sure of making ample net profits in any business—particularly in a retail business handling a multiplicity of articles—is to keep close watch on details.

There are but twenty-four hours in a day. If an idea strikes the average executive and he has within arm's reach the means of verifying its value, he settles the matter at once. But if means of verification are not at hand, if they require "digging," he will hesitate; and if he thinks the interest is of minor importance he, as a rule, will sidetrack the matter in favor of other interests clamoring for attention.

O*VERSTOCKING on slow-moving lines often represents a dead loss in the retail store—automatic restriction of purchases in a chain of shoe houses.*

The situation of the manager in one of a chain of stores in a big organization is the same. He has just so much vital energy, and there is plenty of selling work to absorb it all. But it is of prime importance that he shall spend some of that energy in studying the entire picture of his establishment as the general management sees it. Unless that picture is plainly painted for him, however, with the lights and shadows all filled in, and hung where he can see it merely by raising his eyes, he will not study it. Routine duties crowd it out. To paint

FORM 1: *This is the left half of the "blanket report." The original is fourteen by sixteen inches. The left column in each case represents the current year; the right the corresponding period of the previous year*

just such a picture for each store manager, the following sales and expense record system was designed.

When natural development and expansion had come to

the business—had converted a chain of specialty stores
handling only one-price men's shoes into a chain of general
eral stores selling a comparatively wide variety of mer-

FORM I-A: *This is the right half of the report shown in Form I. The
report brings together monthly and cumulative statistics and compares them
with the previous year*

chandise—it then became necessary to accommodate each
store to local conditions, to scan investment figures more
closely, to favor the more profitable lines, and in a hun-

dred ways to exercise, through the manager, an intelligence such as can be exercised only when a comparative bird's-eye view of condensed details is available.

The problem, then, was to supply hundreds of store managers, men who were keen and able, but who had been trained to do or to think of little else than selling goods, with complete information about their own stores —information covering investment, interest charges, depreciation charges, gross profit, net profit, expense— such information, in short, as a real merchant must have and must use in planning his business moves. Furthermore, the information must be furnished in simple, understandable form, without calling for effort which might distract the manager from his more important duties.

We solved this problem by providing each manager, not with a set of books, but with a single sheet of vellum paper which lasted for one year, and on which appeared, in detail, all the vital figures of his store from month to month—sales, expenses, inventory, and so on. This sheet is shown in Forms I and 1A. In the left column in each case are entered the detailed figures for each month of the preceding fiscal year, together with a running total (of the main items only) for convenience in making comparisons. Each month the figures on each item for the current month are copied in the column at the right. Thus the practical use of this form is made easy for an untrained mind because the figures on the left-hand side all refer to past performances, while those on the white refer to current business.

By this method the store manager has constantly under his eye the source of every dollar of income, the cause of every dollar of outgo, the total investment in stock, in fixtures and in improvements. And he has all these figures placed directly alongside the corresponding figures for the previous year. In fact, he has before him, what, I think I am safe in saying, not one merchant out of twenty-five has before him at any time. And he has it in such shape and so easy to size up that he can utilize any leisure moment to pick up the sheet and get at facts and tendencies at once. No preliminary digging for data is necessary—no mass of reports and tabulations such as the ordinary bookkeeper loves to furnish but which no ordinary store manager has the patience to labor over, or having labored over can easily understand.

♉

IF WE could secure the complete sympathy and cooperation of every person employed in our business operations, it would soon result in the invention, adoption, and complete assimilation of the most up-to-date methods. And without such cooperation, we cannot completely assimilate and economically operate any complete system of modern methods.

—A. W. Burritt

President, A. W. Burritt Company

XIV

RECORDS THAT SAFEGUARD PRINTING ESTIMATES

By Neil M. Clark

ESTIMATES are the basis on which the printer secures work. These estimates, if they are accepted, bind you with the force of a contract, and in your bill to the customer you must live up to your first figure. If you were wrong, if your original estimate was too low and a loss is incurred in doing the work, it falls on your own shoulders. You cannot burden the customer with a charge arising from your own carelessness or ignorance. If you wish to avoid the possibility of grossly wrong estimates, it is essential that you know costs in every department of your business.

Simplicity, the provision that each job shall bear its due proportion of overhead, and the means of quickly tracing errors in estimates—these are the points that distinguish the cost system of one large printing concern recognized as among the foremost. Actual experience has shown that the principles embodied in this system can be applied equally well to the smaller business.

When the order is received, details are copied on the office job record (Form I). This sheet is the real heart of the cost system, since all items comprised in the cost of the job, as well as the details of its history, are gathered together on it. Wide margins at the left allow the sheets to be bound in book form. They are arranged according to order numbers, and immediate reference to any job thus becomes easy. The upper right-hand corner is perforated so that it can be torn off as a sign that the job is finished and posting is completed. A glance through the binder, therefore, shows which orders are finished and billed, and which are still on hand in the shop.

Form II is the reverse of this office job record sheet. Details of cost, gathered from day to day, are entered in the proper columns, including the date and, as in the case of the press room, the number of the machine used; or, as in the composing room, the kind of work done. These details are secured from the time tickets of the various departments.

Composing room and press room tickets are shown in Forms III and IV. The workman indicates by a letter the kind of work he is doing, puts the job number in the proper column and crosses out the times of starting and stopping. Other departments have time tickets made up in the same style, differing only in the details. For small shops, it has been found unnecessary to have more than one ticket. Such a ticket can easily be made with special columns, one for the composing room, another for the platen press room, a third for the cylinder press room and a fourth for the bindery, with other columns if they are needed. If your bookkeeping force is small, one form saves time in the office.

After all details for the job are complete, the columns on Form II are totaled and transferred to the "costs" column of Form I. Other details for this column are obtained from invoices, in the case of work or stock bought on the outside, and from stock requisitions.

Overhead is also distributed in this "cost" column.

FORM I: *The office job record contains the complete history of each job and a record of all costs connected with it.   When the job is finished, the corner is torn off to indicate this fact*

Percentage on wages is the method used in this distribution. Two percentages are figured in each department: one for charges which vary; one for fixed charges. The first percentage includes such items as superintendence, all indirect labor, idle time and sundries which vary from week to week. The second percentage is for rent, depreciation, interest on investment and other fixed charges. Thus, if direct wages on a certain job in the composing room are $2.00, and the overhead percentages for that department have been fixed at 20% and 30% respectively, then $0.40 and $0.60 are charged for composing room overhead. The same process is fol-

FORM II: *Reverse of Form I, showing how the details of cost are recorded from day to day for every job, giving finally the totals by headings*

lowed in press room and bindery, with different percentages.

After total costs for the shop have been collected, two more percentages, figured on the basis of total shop cost, are added to complete the distribution of overhead. First is a small percentage for boxing and shipping, and

second a larger percentage which distributes general
office, selling and administrative expense. Thus, if the
total shop cost on a certain job is found to be $8.00, and
the shipping and selling percentages for the current year

FORMS III and IV: The former (front card) is the time ticket used in
the composing room.   Form IV is the platen press time ticket. Each kind
of work has a symbol, which is entered in the last column

are 2% and 30% respectively, then $0.16 and $2.40 are
added to the $8.00. Commission, car fare and other in-
cidental expenses connected with the job are included,
giving the complete cost. A comparison of this figure
with the estimate shows how nearly correct the latter
was and gives a line on the accuracy of solicitors and
the efficiency of operating departments; comparison with
the billed price to the customer shows the amount of gain
or loss on the job, and furnishes the immediate basis for
bringing together overhead percentages and estimates.

As each job is finished, the details are posted from

the office job record to the journal, in which each job has a line across a large page, and the individual costs for each department and kind of work are posted to the proper columns. In this way it is possible to secure total costs for each department and kind of work for a month, year, or any period desired, and percentages are deduced which are invaluable in estimating future jobs.

Division of overhead has been brought to so nice an adjustment, that actual costs in this concern vary from the amounts charged to specific jobs by not more than 1 or 2% a year. Particularly valuable is the system, also, because of the fact that it fits in with the general accounting system; is really an essential part of it. The facts collected enable the printer to do away with guess work in his estimates. The shop, in short, is run on a basis of accurate knowledge.

MODERN scientific management is exactly what the name implies—management based on knowledge—on ascertained facts rather than on opinions, however brilliant—of workman, foreman, superintendent or manager.

—S. B. Peck

Vice-President, Link Belt Company

XV

COSTS IN A PROFESSIONAL OFFICE

By O. M. Biggar

PROFESSIONAL costs are generally kept with little pretense of accuracy. Very often the doctor, lawyer or dentist charges what he thinks the client can afford to pay, rather than what the job is actually worth. That the office which carries this to the extreme drives away trade goes without saying. The nearer you can fix charges on a basis of actual cost, and the more equitably you apportion them among all your customers, so much the better are your chances of retaining and increasing the volume of your business.

In establishing a law office on a business foundation, one of the members of a western firm of attorneys decided to ascertain the cost of each piece of business in the office and so have a basis for determining what fees each client should pay; not necessarily so that the cost should be the only factor, but so that the cost should be at least one of the factors. The importance and urgency of the business, the amount of money involved, and in many cases the ability of the client to pay, all enter into the final determination of the charge to be made. But while in almost every other business the cost of doing the work is a prime factor in determining the charge, in law the cost is usually altogether unknown, and charges are often made in complete ignorance of it.

Clients are frequently very keen judges of the ease or difficulty with which their affairs can be adjusted and, in the early stages of their connection with a law firm, may be estranged by a charge which seems out of proportion with the services rendered.

ESTABLISHING *a system of cost keeping in a law office resulted in better work on the part of employees and more equitable charges to clients.*

Any one with office experience knows also that clerks and investigators are likely to make much more effective use of their hours if called upon to account for them daily. On this score of individual efficiency alone, a time and cost keeping system is worth more than the expense of operating it and checking up its workings at intervals.

Considerations like these led to the abandonment of rule-of-thumb methods in the office in question and brought about the development of a system which not only safeguards the interests of the firm, but also insures the placing of equitable charges against clients for services rendered, thus putting the transaction on a business basis.

The first requirement was to provide for a record of original charges. The solution of the problem was a slip that contains a space for the file number—every matter has a file and each is numbered—and spaces for the time at which the work on the particular matter was begun and finished. This slip is shown in Form I. The rest of the card (which is seven by eight and a half inches in size and is printed on common news print) contains printed matter to facilitate the notation of the work by simply drawing a cross through the proper words, as shown in the accompanying illustration. A blank space at the bottom provides for special memoranda wherever the task is outside ordinary routine or has been attended with unusual difficulty.

These time slips are arranged to care for every individual in the office, except members of the bookkeeping

FORM I: *Each worker in the office keeps a daily record of work done on each case by simply running his pencil through the items that occupied his time*

and filing staff, and each individual's slips are distinguished by his number. These slips are filled in from moment to moment through the day. The principals keep record of their own time when they are engaged with clients, but the stenographers keep the principals' time, together with their own, and fill in slips for the principals as well as for themselves while they are engaged in taking dictation. These daily time slips thus containing a record of the whole day's work, are collected by the cost clerk, who first stamps on them the date, and then enters on special monthly cards (Form II) the total time consumed by each individual. A small memorandum is filled in to show how much time each person consumed in accomplishing the tasks of the previous day. These are distributed to the individuals concerned and, unless an explanation is called for, he makes a note of how he spent his working hours and destroys them. Should the slip show an error in office record he notifies the cost clerk and the correction is made.

After the total time spent by the individual has been entered, the original slips are distributed behind guide

NO.	DAILY RECORD							MONTH OF	
DATE	HOURS	DATE	HOURS	DATE	HOURS	DATE	HOURS		
1		9		17		25			
2		10		18		26		TOTAL HOURS DUE	
3		11		19		27			
4		12		20		28			
5		13		21		29			
6		14		22		30		HOURS WORKED	
7		15		23		31			
8		16		24					
FWD.		FWD.		FWD.		TOTAL			

FORM II: *The time of each person in the office is entered daily on this card. The number of hours constituting a full month's work is standardized, and continual deficiency or excess results in a rearrangement*

cards that bear the file numbers. Thus behind each guide card a series of slips contains a complete record of all work done on each case, in the original handwriting of the person who did the work, with the day and time when the work was done. Whenever it becomes necessary to render a detailed bill the slips give more information in more convenient shape for reference than the old docket method could possibly furnish.

The salary paid to each junior and clerk is of course known, and the members of the firm themselves determine their salary, acting on the assumption that they

FILE NO.					MONTHLY RECORD					FROM				
CLIENT			RE							TO				
NO.	TIME	FAC.	COST	DISB.	NO.	TIME	FAC.	COST	DISB.	NO.	TIME	FAC.	COST	DISB.
1					FWD					A1				
2					17					A2				

MONTHLY SALARY OVERHEAD CALCULATION															
			FOR MONTH OF										191		
NO.	SALARY	VALUE TIME WORKED	NO.	SALARY	VALUE TIME WORKED	NO.	SALARY	VALUE TIME WORKED	NO.	SALARY	VALUE TIME WORKED				
1			17												
2			18												
3			19												
4			20												
5			21												
6			22												
7			23												
8			24												
9			25												
10			26												
11			27												
12			28												
13			29												
14			30												
15			31												
16			32												

FORM III (upper sheet): The cost of one piece of business is entered monthly on this card. FORM IV (lower sheet): The difference between standard and actual time goes from this card to "overhead"

are merely hired managers of the business. The time value of every office worker is thus ascertained, and once every month the cost of each piece of business is brought up to date on a card printed especially for the purpose (Form III). The slips collected up to date

MONTHLY OVERHEAD CALCULATION FOR MONTH OF _____ 191__

PARTICULARS	HEAD OFFICE	BRANCH A	BRANCH B	BRANCH C	BRANCH D	REMARKS
SALARIES LESS VALUE OF TIME WORKED						
RENT						
LIGHT						
TELEPHONE						
INSURANCE						
PROPORTION OF BAD ACCTS.						
PROPORTION OF DEPRECIATION.						
PROPORTION OF TAXES						
LOSSES AND SUNDRIES						
STATIONERY						
ADVERTISING						
PRIVATE AND OVERHEAD						
TOTAL						
VALUE OF TIME WORKED						
OVERHEAD %						

ANALYSIS AND SUMMARY.

FILE NO. _____   RE _____ TO _____ 191

CLIENT _____

	HEAD OFFICE		BRANCH A		BRANCH B		BRANCH C		BRANCH D	
	TIME	DISB.	TIME	DISB.	TIME	DISB.	TIME	DISB.	TIME	DISB.
TIME, COST AND DISB.										
OVERHEAD @ 70%										
TOTAL FOR MONTH										
FOR'D. FROM LAST SHEET										
TOTAL TO DATE										

FORM V (upper sheet): Overhead expense items other than indirect labor, are entered on this card every month. FORM VI (lower sheet): This card when filled out gives the total cost of a case of this card are then filed away until the conclusion of the matter, when reference to them may be necessary.

At the end of every month the bookkeeper prepares a salary overhead card (Form IV) from the data shown on Form II. The difference between the time actually charged to each person and the time which would represent a full month's work is charged to the "overhead" account, and the total is swelled by the salaries of bookkeepers, filing clerks, boys and other employees who are not directly engaged on particular pieces of business.

This salary overhead is carried to the general monthly overhead card shown in Form V, which includes a summary of all overhead expenses for the period. The time charged as the work of members to specific matters is written off at once, and allowance is made for bad debts. A percentage of overhead expense is then attained, and provision is made for adding this overhead monthly to the cost of each individual case by entering a due percentage on a special form printed on the back of Form III and illustrated in Form VI. The actual cost is thus known and the total from the last monthly card is brought forward to this card. Having the actual costs of any case always at hand, it is a simple matter to make equitable charges by adding whatever percentage of profit seems fair under the circumstances. If a detailed bill is desired, the itemized material for it is on the original slips, and although the relations between lawyers and their clients are based essentially on confidence, there is no question but that the reduction of charges to a basis similar to that in use in every commercial business rivets the faith and good will of clients to the firm.

This system has two further advantages: By carrying the total of the monthly cards into a loose-leaf record book from month to month, a "work in process" account may be opened in the ledger, and the exact standing of the firm on any balance day thus ascertained. Again, if it appears from this book that nothing has been done in a specific case since the last monthly record card was made up, a "signal" sheet calls attention to the matter. This signal sheet is of red paper to differentiate it from ordinary case sheets. On it appear in rotation the file number, the time cost and disbursements to date, and the announcement, "Nothing has been charged in this file for a month. Please close." This is handed to the partner in charge, so that the account may be rendered. Sim-

TIME AND EXPENSE RECORD FOR WEEK ENDING SEE OTHER SIDE												191
OWNER OF ORDER	M	T	W	T	F	S	OT.	HRS. TOTAL	AMT.	CASH EX.	DRY MAT	MISC.
TOTAL												
RECEIVED $	IN FULL			FOR TIME AND CASH EXPENSE								
SIGNED												
FROM JAMES A. DAWSON, ARCHITECTS												

FORM VII: On this card, used by every person in an architect's office, are entered daily reports of time spent, material used and cash expenses. The card covers one week

plicity without complication in details forms the basis of the system, and this firm has learned that equitable charges founded on accurate knowledge win the good will of clients to such an extent that the slight extra labor and expense are more than offset.

Applied to other professional lines, the same care in

cost keeping will show proportionate results. A large architectural firm in the middle west gathers all cost items having to do with labor or materials on a single card (Form VII), which serves also as a receipt for wages and other cash expenses incurred by the worker and chargeable against the business. This compact card is used by every member of the concern—draftsman, building superintendent or stenographer—and covers a period of one week. Items are posted from it to the proper job, wage, material and expense accounts in the ledger. The card forms the basis of an effective cost system, placing every charge where it belongs.

Doctor, dentist or lawyer, whatever the nature of the professional services you offer, you can adapt a modified cost system to your needs. Having such a system in satisfactory working order, you may feel assured that the equitable distribution of charges resulting will bring increased satisfaction among your clients, and the natural consequences of better and bigger business.

A SPIRIT *of cooperation means "team work," and something more. It is a real and a great force; it is to the business house what "college spirit" is to a university, esprit de corps to a regiment, civic pride to a city and patriotism to a nation.*

—Leslie H. Thompson

XVI

HOW A BANKER FIGURED
HIS COSTS

By Harry N. Grut

A BANKER telephoned to one of his commercial depositors, "Drop in when you are going by here to-day or tomorrow. I've just been looking over the monthly statement of your balance and want to see you about it. We lost money on your account last month."

The depositor came over post-haste—and brought with him his balance statement for the preceding month. It showed an average daily balance of $20,000. Triumphantly, he laid it on the banker's desk.

"You were looking over some other man's account when you called me up," he said. "You can't be losing money on my account. I'll bet it's one of the best you've got—I carry a balance of $20,000."

Then the banker laid before the depositor an analysis of his account—really a cost sheet—that opened his eyes on the subject of banking; on what a balance really means and what it costs a bank to do business. What the depositor really saw was the bank's cost system—made up of credit and debit items just as is the cost sheet of a factory; based on a tabulation of items, of the cost of handling each account just as a factory's costs are built on individual time tickets and individual requisition items. And such a system is just as necessary in a bank —to show the banker his cost of doing business, to prevent him from losing money, to keep him in profitable lines—as it is for the manufacturer or merchant.

As the customer glanced over the sheet, the banker explained his viewpoint. "It is true," he said, "you had for the past month a daily average balance of $20,000. Nevertheless, this statement shows a loss of $7.13 and an examination of the account for three months shows a loss of from $5 to $10."

The depositor gazed on the statement in bewilderment. That he could have a daily average of $20,000 and yet have the bank lose money on the account was inconsistent with his business experience. The president, appreciating how little the average depositor knows of the actual methods and practices of a bank, went on with his explanation:

"The out-of-town items in process of collection or in transit for the month amounted to $10,000. This left a balance of $10,000, and after deducting our legal reserve fund of 25 per cent, there was a net balance of $7,500. In other words, out of an average balance of $20,000, we have available for loans only $7,500."

"Even so," protested the depositor, "I don't see how you can figure a loss of $7.13—or any loss at all." •

"You will note,"—the banker with pencil in hand was pointing to certain items on the analysis report—"that we paid you 2 per cent on the $20,000, or $33.38, for the month. Our operating expenses on the account totaled $15.00 so that the actual cost to us of handling the business was $48.38.

"Now, for our earnings: We loaned the $7,500 at 5 per cent, which brought us in $31.25 for the month, and $10 more can be added as exchange on collections. You see where the $7.13 loss comes in? It is a simple matter of subtracting the earnings from the expenses."

The depositor studied the figures in silence for several minutes.

"Am I to understand," he finally asked, "that it will be necessary for me to increase my daily average very materially in order that you may make a profit on my account?"

"Yes—and no. The balance should be increased or it might be possible for you to adopt some method for quickening your transactions; reduce the time now required for handling out-of-town items—in a word, crystallize your balances more quickly."

"But how much of a daily balance ought I to carry?"

"Well, suppose it were $50,000. Here is the way it would figure out: Deducting the $10,000 in out-of-town items and the 25 per cent reserve would leave $30,000 available for loaning. At 5 per cent it would bring us in $125 for the month and the exchange would easily add $15 more, or $140 earnings."

"The 2 per cent we pay you on the $50,000 amounts to $83.33 and the operating expenses would not exceed $20, or a total of $103.33. You see, we have a net profit on the account of $36.67."

EXCHANGE *and operating costs may swallow up the bank's profit on an active account—cost sheets enable the banker to establish a line of safety.*

The banker cannot take for granted any item or account, no matter how profitable it may look to the outsider. Like the manufacturer or the merchant, he must know exactly what it costs him to perform a certain service and just what his margin of profit is—and the information must be laid before him at frequent intervals, enabling him to take steps to stop a leakage and help the depositor to quicken up a losing account, so that the bank can afford to handle it on a permanent basis.

A line of safety must be established for every account —a variable line that must be watched as it rises and falls from month to month. On one side of the line is a balance sufficient to cover all commercial requirements; on the other side a loanable balance of sufficient size to make the account profitable.

Each year the size of the daily balances is a little larger on account of the growing practice among merchants of sending personal checks drawn on their local banks in settlement of obligations, instead of using current exchange. The result is that items placed in transit for collection each day must be deducted from the customers' daily balance.

A merchant, for example, in Aberdeen, South Dakota, sends a check drawn on a local bank to the wholesale house in Chicago. It takes four and a half days at the best to clear the check, and during this time the Chicago banker deducts the amount from the wholesaler's daily balance. Such items, in large numbers, play havoc with the loanable value of the account and necessitate the larger daily balance.

To determine what the balance of each customer must be to make his account profitable requires a careful analysis that, with the larger banks, has resulted in the organization of a separate department. Every account is examined three times a month, at intervals of ten days. At the end of the month summaries are made and laid before the president so that the executive can get in touch with the depositor whose business is unprofitable and point out to him what steps must be taken if he desires to continue his banking relations with that particular institution.

The analysis embraces three items: the average daily

SKETCH ANALYSIS RECORDS — FROM ——— TO ———

DEPOSITOR ———

DATES	A. M. C. H.	P. M. C. H.	NEW YORK	TRANSIT	EXCHANGE RECEIVED	EXCHANGE COST	DESCRIPTION.
26							
27							
28							
29							
30							
31							
1							
2							
3							
4							
5							
6							
7							
8							
9							
10							
11							
12							
13							
14							
15							
26							
TOTALS							

FORM I: On this card the account of each depositor is carefully analyzed, so that it can be laid periodically on the executive's desk for scrutiny balance, the average daily amount in transit and the daily loanable balance. Figures for the first item are obtained by taking the actual balance as shown on the ledger for each day during the month, adding the amounts and dividing the total by the number of days.

The deposits of whatever account is under analysis are recorded on a separate sheet (Form I), ruled with columns for the different classes. First are entered the checks on Chicago deposited in time for clearing. These are treated as cash. In the second column are entered the checks on Chicago received in the afternoon, too late to be cleared before the following day. Next are shown the checks on New York City, and then the checks on miscellaneous points throughout the country; columns are also provided for the amounts of exchange paid by the depositors and the cost of exchange to the bank.

At the end of the month, the total amount in transit is divided by the number of days in the month, thus showing the daily average in transit.

A NALYSIS *of each customer's account must be accurate and thorough, for the margin of profit in the bank's business is often extremely narrow.*

This form was adopted after several years' experimenting and does away with the laborious method formerly in use of listing each item according to the amount of exchange and again listing it according to the time for clearing.

The difference between the items in transit or uncollected funds and the average daily balance (less the legal reserve) gives the banker the loanable balance. And that the figures may be accurate, the exact cost of each operation is figured. The man in charge of the analysis takes three months of the regular business for every

FORM II: *The cost analysis report reaches the executive head on this form, and he knows at once whether the danger limit has been reached* banking point in the country, figuring the actual exchange cost and dividing it by the volume received during the period for each point. In arriving at the average cost per thousand of exchange, and where the business for any one point is too small to warrant a flat rate, the cost is based on each item.

In completing the analysis, the banker takes into his reckoning the cost of exchange on out-of-town items, the interest paid on daily balances, the cost of transfers (this usually represents the market value of New York in Chicago, which is an item that will most likely vary with all banks), and the general operating expenses. In figuring his overhead, the banker totals all his expenses except interest on balances—which is figured separately in each case—and divides this total by the average daily deposits for the year. The result shows the average rate per cent the business costs for the year.

In making the calculations the deduction covering funds in New York is omitted, for the items vary with all banks. In the one bank's practice the average yearly balances kept in New York banks are divided by the average deposits for the year, deducting from the average balances with the bank of the account under analysis the per cent thus obtained and crediting the interest received on i: as being carried in New York for the use of that account.

This brings the analysis up to the point where it shows the loanable value of the account. From the average daily balance is subtracted the average daily amount in transit, together with charges thereon, and then the 25 per cent legal reserve must be taken out and the remainder is the amount left to be loaned.

The completed analytical report as laid before the president (Form II) is as follows:

Clearing house items $54,000
Out-of-town items 86,900

Daily average balance on basis of remitting
   down to $25,000 44,500
Less daily loanable total in transit . . . 11,000

                                                  $33,500
Less 25 per cent reserve 8,375

                                                  $25,125

Value thirty days at 5 per cent $104.68
Exchange paid to bank 34.70

Total receipts $139.38

Interest at 2 per cent for 30 days . . . $ 63.80
Exchange cost 34.70
Cost New York Exchange 15.70
Cost of operating 30.00

Total expense $144.20

Bank received $139.38
Bank paid out 144.20

Bank lost . . . . $ 4.82

This report brings before the president of the bank the fact that it was losing $4.82 a month and it was for him to suggest to the depositor some readjustment that would either reduce the amount of the items in transit or increase the average daily balance from $44,500 to a point that would show a profit. If the items were confined to the one bank or even to local banks, very likely an increase in daily balances would be unnecessary. If the out-of-town accounts were liquidated by current exchange, the customer would have a smaller amount charged against his balance. These expense analyses, corresponding to the cost sheet in a factory, bring before the banker in forcible and simple shape, the places where his business is weak and where it is strong, where it is making money and where it is losing.

IN BUSINESS *the earning of profit is something more than an incident of success. It is an essential condition of success, because the continued absence of profit itself spells failure. But while loss spells failure, large profits do not connote success. Success must be sought in business also in excellence of performance; and in business, excellence of performance manifests itself, among other things, in the advancing of methods and processes; in the improvement of products; in more perfect organization, eliminating friction as well as waste; in bettering the condition of the working-men, developing their faculties and promoting their happiness; and in the establishment of right relations with customers and with the community.*

—Louis D. Brandeis

PART IV—USING GRAPHS AS STATISTICS IN BUSINESS

When Your Market Expands

AMERICA and most American markets are growing rapidly. When facing a rapidly expanding market remember these six bits of wisdom:

1. To watch out for the danger of over-expanding manufacturing facilities.

2. To break up the market into detailed, definite opportunities.

3. To pick out from among these opportunities those that can be sold with the least effort and to the greatest advantage—shake the tree for the ripe ones first, in other words, before you try to climb it for the others.

4. Analyze the specific requirements of each one of these opportunities.

5. Fit the advantageous qualities of the product to the requirements.

6. Tell those who have these requirements all about the way in which the product fits them.

ALBERT Y. GOWEN

Vice-President, the Lehigh Portland Cement Company

XVII

BEHIND THE FIGURES

By A. E. Andersen

AN UNEXPLAINED shortage of $15,000 in the raw material account for the year just closed led the general manager of a specialty concern through the sales, purchasing, cost and operating departments to the little registering device at the side of each finishing machine.

The product was sold by the lineal foot. The figures indicated that the material used exceeded by $15,000 worth what had been delivered to customers. No "bookkeeping errors" were found, but when the accuracy of the records had been checked and proved, the reason for the loss was found in the devices for registering the quantity of product turned out. These were out of order. For more than a year every customer had been charged for much less than had actually been shipped because the counters had "slipped." Since the gifts were of finished product the loss was nearly double the cost of the raw material.

Right figures check, guide and control any business. A suitable accounting system, matched to the size and needs of the business, throws to the surface significant facts. More—it brings to the man at the head of the business, grouped and related details which otherwise would escape attention. A market man in Massachusetts learns from his records of what people are buying, when he ought to push fish instead of meat, or pork instead of mutton. He is getting behind his figures, just as is the manufacturer in Chicago who sets quotas of sales and output based on what has been sold and made in the past and asks "why?" when the monthly reports fluctuate either below or above the figures set. No matter what your business may be, you can set your accounting to watch the significant factors in that business.

VITAL *facts which show the up or down tendencies of a business can only be secured by going behind the bare figures and reading their true meaning.*

Different managers have different methods of finding these significant facts. What some men sense by experience others get from tabulated and charted facts. A factory cost accountant put in a rather elaborate system for the superintendent. He collected the costs of steel for the blade, the wood for the handle, the labor and overhead expenses in making a kitchen knife. After he had collected figures for a couple of months, the superintendent of the plant took a note book out of his pocket and said that they agreed pretty closely with what he had figured as the costs on the different grades.

The superintendent knew by long experience the average total cost of certain classes of orders. But when the cost man went over his tabulated figures and showed him the relative department charges for overhead expenses, he brought to the superintendent's attention a fact which he had not before realized—that he was losing money on certain classes of goods. Only by department comparisons could such a condition come to light.

A suitable cost system in a manufacturing plant may show one manager the significant facts in his business. Figures may prophesy in a merchandising establishment,

when the records are planned to control the business.
The sales manager of a large jewelry house with an extensive local and country business has a plan for knowing

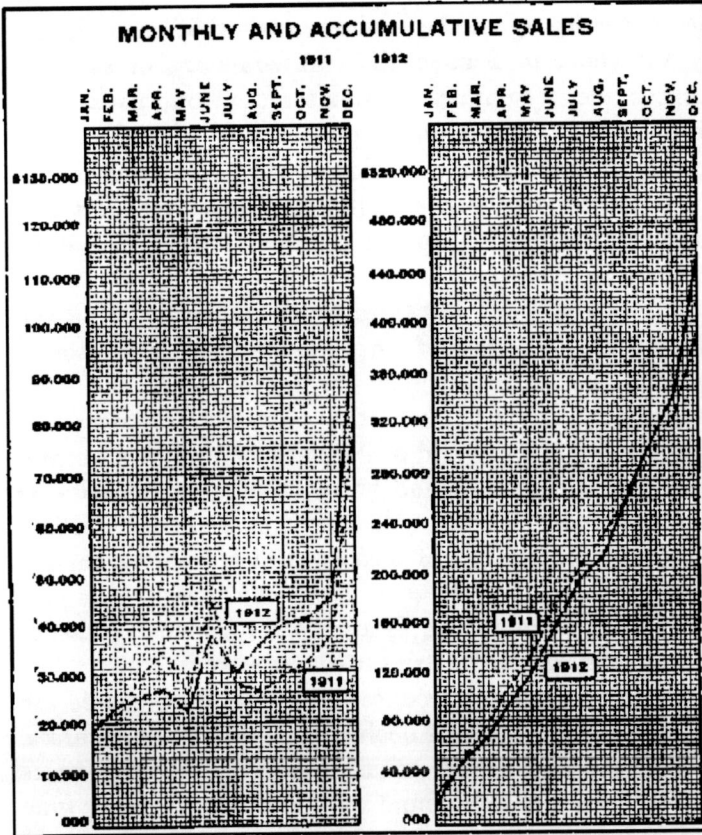

FIGURE VII: *The chart on the left showed one manager a slump in
sales.   The reason was an advertising campaign which started too late.
The right-hand section shows cumulative sales for two years*

what is going on, which is adaptable to other lines. Like
other executives, he has found that charts showing gross
sales both in quantities and money values will enable him

to know definitely what the sales department is doing in each line and will direct him to the weak spots in his organization.

Returning on one occasion from a trip abroad, he found conditions in the business somewhat as indicated by the chart in Figure VII. A summary of sales by months and accumulative sales for the same period had been contrasted with the corresponding figures for the corresponding month or period of the previous year. At the beginning of January quite an extensive advertising campaign had been prepared. He had looked for a large increase in sales.

But as the chart indicates, when he returned on the last of May, instead of an increase there had been a gradual decline in business for the current year. Investigation showed that the advertising campaign planned to start the first of January had not been begun until late in March. Had he not compared his sales he would not have learned at once the cause of the decline. As it was, the increase of business which is shown for the months of July and August on the charts was made possible by the prompt application of additional pressure on the sales and advertising departments.

Records of this sort reduced to a unit basis enable the managers of all kinds of businesses to watch their courses. Statements and charts which show the average price realized per ton, per pound or per barrel by steel, glue and brewing companies, enable the sales managers of these respective concerns to keep in touch with the results obtained by each salesman. Similarly the pay rolls of large retail stores are watched. A record is kept of each clerk's business, day by day. Each week the percentage of salaries to the sales made is calculated. At any time the superintendent and department manager know what the pay roll stands for in sales, and which clerks are efficient.

Whenever a business man, at the end of the year or the month, sits at his desk with the figures of the period before him, one of the obvious things he watches is the

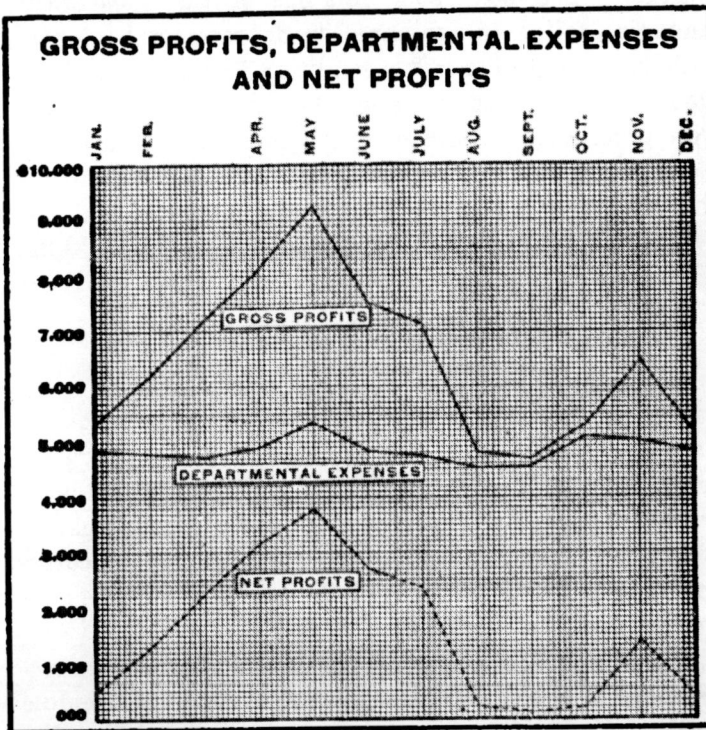

GROSS PROFITS, DEPARTMENTAL EXPENSES AND NET PROFITS

FIGURE VIII: This chart showed one dealer the close interdependence of his gross and net profits, and expenses. Note how the failure to reduce expenses during August and September nearly consumed net profits

relation between expenses and the amount of business done. His records must be planned to show comparative statements and charts of sales, cost of sales, expenses and net profits. Unless the figures get to him in this form it is difficult to see how the outlay matches up with the amount of business done.

An interesting example which indicates how the vice-president of a wholesale house follows gross profits and departmental expenses is shown in Figure VIII. Trade conditions had been poor and one of the department managers failed to compare his departmental expense with his gross profits. This condition continued until the month of August when, as will be seen, the gross profits were practically consumed by the departmental expense. Each month now this department head gets his comparative statement of gross profits and departmental expenses and does not wait for the figures to ''push'' him. He pushes the figures.

FIGURES *are of no value in and of themselves—interpretation by the executive is necessary if they are made to reveal their inner significance.*

Tradition says figures do not lie. Yet, the wrong interpretation of figures may throw the head of the business completely off the track. Groups of facts must be considered with relation to the right groups of corresponding facts. Both sides of the question must be considered in the tabulated statistics.

A sash and door company began to scrutinize the records of its twelve salesmen, mostly young and middle aged men. The low gross sales of one of the older salesmen at first led the president to believe that this older man was being kept on the pay roll for sentimental reasons. But when he took the sales records of the various products and compared them with the profits obtained on each sale he changed his mind. He found that while the older man sold less in the aggregate than his fellow travelers, the total profit on his business was greater.

Because of his experience, he knew the profitable and unprofitable lines. The comparison of the two sets of figures showed how the company had gone wrong and a new sales policy was inaugurated at once. Every salesman was instructed to concentrate effort on the profitable lines, and allow the low-profit lines to sell themselves or use them to push the more profitable specialties.

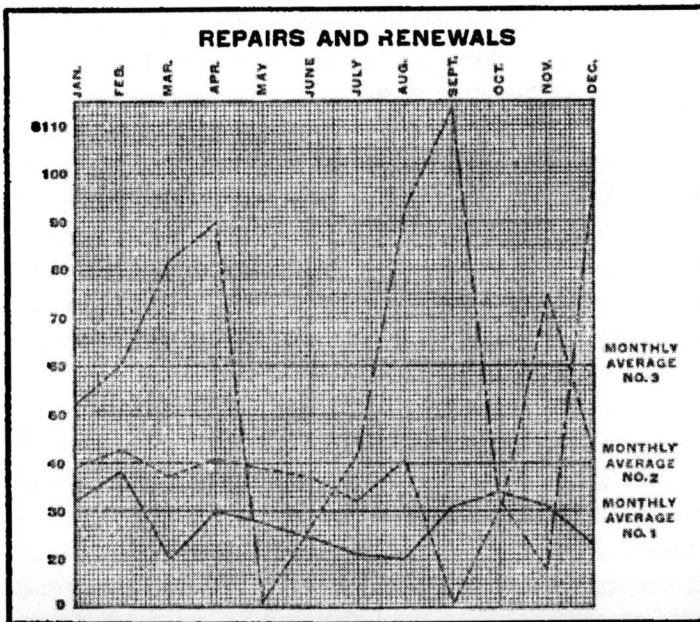

FIGURE IX: *This comparison of the repairs and renewals required by three mining machines brought to attention the abuse of No. 3 and resulted in hiring a more careful operator for it*

Look into any group of figures for the significant items; the records of one department compared with the others or of one branch compared with the next will often suggest a more uniformly profitable way of handling the business. Lumped figures do not show tendencies. A poor machine in one department may keep up the total relative cost of the output of that department. One slow line of goods may distort the figures of a store. It is better to individualize accounts wherever possible in order that each may stand on its own merits.

The president of a mining company suspected that his repair and renewal account was higher than it should be, purely because of his general knowledge of conditions. Not until he had compared the expenditures for repairs and renewals on three machines, as shown in Figure IX, did he realize that two of the machines had suffered unjustly for the faults of one. The three cutting machines were of the same general design and cost and were installed about the same time. When the facts came out that machine Number 3 had much greater repair and renewal expense than the other two, it was discovered that the man who had charge of this machine subjected it to much rougher usage than the operator of either of the other two machines.

Figures that mean most to the head of a business must contain all the elements entering into a consideration of any particular item. Statements and charts of sales and expenses only without cost of goods sold may prove misleading. Business is done for profit, not for sales totals. Two concerns may be doing substantially the same gross business; one, however, may be doing its greater business at a much higher cost.

The Philadelphia and Baltimore offices of an electrical supply house had substantially the same total of sales. Yet, when the annual statement came in it was found that much more money was made in one office than in the other in spite of the fact that the volume of sales was about the same in both. When the figures came to the general manager of the company, he saw at once that the reason Baltimore netted less in profits than Philadelphia was two-fold: supplies had been sold at too close a margin of profit and sales and office salaries were disproportionate to the amount of business done.

Often by matching department with department, branch office with branch office, machine with machine or clerk with clerk, a better understanding can be obtained of what the business is doing. It has been found in many businesses that comparative expense statements, furnished to branch managers with the comments of an executive officer, will do much to hold down cost. On the second Tuesday of each month, the manager of a soda-fountain business devotes his entire day to the study of statements and graphic charts. Sales, branch and departmental expenses and other elements entering into profit and loss accounts come under his supervision. One of the reasons why the company can do business at a low cost is because the manager knows how to use the figures in his business.

COMPARISON *of results in different branches of a business, or different departments, often reveals to the executive places where leaks are occurring.*

Studying a statement itemizing the expenses of one of the larger branches of the company, the head noticed that the wages of the unloading and shipping department increased in the four months ending April 30th over a similar cost for the slack season of the previous year. Investigation developed that the manager of the branch had failed to cut, from eight to six, the men in his receiving department.

Receiving and shipping expenses at the Kansas City branch, greater than the average shipping expenses of the seven or eight other branches, drew attention to another condition which might not have come to the manager's notice. Inquiry showed that the receiving and storage facilities were inadequate, that it was necessary to handle material twice in unloading and storing, that the bins, shelves and general layout were poor. By spending five hundred dollars for the improvement of the storeroom, the company made an annual saving of sixteen hundred dollars in this particular item of expense.

Just as a sales manager may get from his records definite knowledge of his sales and profits, so the manufacturer can devise intelligent summaries of expenses that will show him the relative costs of his products. Overhead expenses often go up mysteriously. Unless the expenses are put on paper in comparative form, it is hard to get behind the totals and find out just what is causing the increase in expense. Non-productive labor, salaries of timekeepers, order and shop clerks and supplies consumed, are all details which the head needs to group in such form that ready comparisons may be made.

Itemized, comparative figures make it possible to find the reason for high overhead expenses in the monthly statement of a business. Bulk totals, unless seen in relation to other figures, have little significance unless the man who watches the returns keeps the basic figures in the back of his head, and compares the bulk total with that. Last year's figures may generally be taken as a basis for this year's total. Monthly quotas of expenses sometimes are best. Variations from standard can then be checked before a wrong policy is established. The cost of lubricants in one mine showed a marked increase over the corresponding period of the previous year. When the superintendent investigated he found that the machine operators were burning lubricating oil costing thirty cents a gallon in their torches instead of six-cent illuminating oil.

To check the previous waste, each machine operator was allotted two gallons of oil per day, although an additional quantity could be had by giving reasons. A second cause for the high lubricating cost was caught by watching the amount of money received for oil barrels returned. The credit item for returned barrels seemed smaller than the year before. It developed that the miners, instead of tapping a barrel, had been knocking in the head and filling their pails by dipping into the barrel. About six hundred dollars a year was saved by stopping this practice.

Comparative statements of factory expenses are always instructive. In one case when such figures came to the attention of the manager, an increase of $834.25 in miscellaneous materials and supplies uncovered an important source of waste. The foreman of Department A had in his charge a large stock of materials and supplies, many of which were used in Department B. Unknown to the former, the head of Department B had taken and used wastefully large quantities of material, thinking that the other foreman would have difficulty in explaining the large debit difference in his material account. Two little columns of figures brought out this badly organized spot in the factory where inefficiency existed because of the jealous rivalry of these two foremen.

All sorts of items in overhead expense can be cared for if the totals come before the manager not in the form of bulk figures but itemized under separate headings. The electric-power-used item in one large manufacturing concern totaled $42,300 for one year. In going over the figures, the manager of the plant thought here was an item which would cost more next year because he expected an increase in the business and power used would increase almost in proportion to an increase in production.

OVERHEAD, *material costs, productive and non-productive labor—figures properly displayed and rightly read will show abnormal features in these items.*

The totals stopped him. They looked big for the work already done. He went through the plant and made some rough estimates of apparent wastes in power here and there. Then he talked over the situation with his electrical engineer. He found that by overhauling his wiring, individual meters could be put into the different departments and so the expense of current used in each shop determined. The manager invested nine thousand dollars in these changes. And the first ten months of the current year indicated that in spite of an increase of fifteen per cent in production over the preceding year the total power cost would be, roughly, thirty-two thousand dollars. The saving in power alone the first year would pay for the changes made in the power equipment.

Just as properly displayed and grouped figures will show the rise and fall in manufacturing expenses, so they will indicate to the factory superintendent the inter-relation between productive and non-productive labor—the totals watched most jealously in every manufacturing plant, since every manager knows the necessity of keeping down the ratio between non-productive and productive labor. The relative importance of these items escaped one manager until he plotted his figures in a chart like that shown in Figure X. Put in this graphic way, the increase in non-productive labor for April, 1911, was apparent at a glance. When the foreman of the department was asked for an explanation it was found that two skilled workmen had been kept on the pay roll during a slack period in order that the men would be available when business increased.

Such records are history. The money had been spent. But it was easy to establish a policy that thereafter the foreman should not settle such questions himself but should confer with the superintendent. In this case it was found that the particular men on this work could

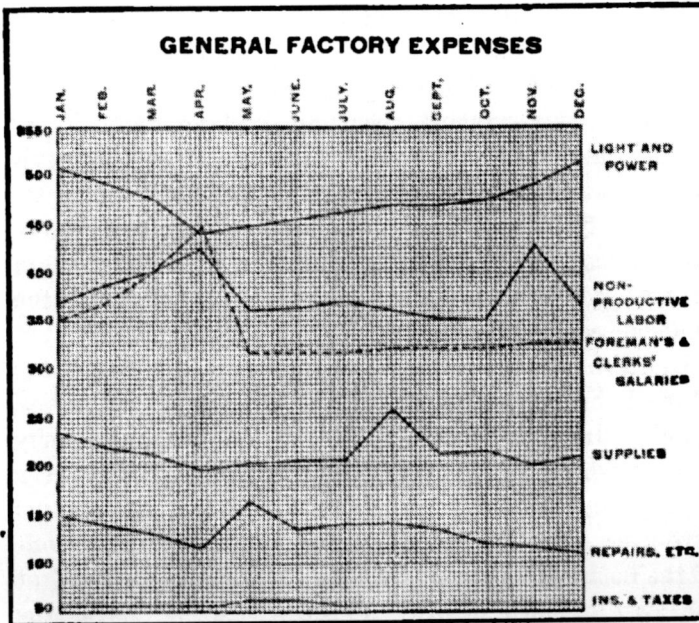

GENERAL FACTORY EXPENSES

FIGURE X: How unusual expenditures can be corrected by a graphic monthly analysis is shown here. Note how the April "peak" in foreman's and clerks' salaries was brought down and kept at a reasonable level

have been easily replaced, although in all instances this might not have been the case. In November of the same year, that chart shows non-productive labor in Department C increased nearly one hundred dollars. The figures were prophecy, not history, for when the manager went behind them he found that they represented an increase in truckers to carry out a different method of moving and shifting merchandise which was not necessary.

> CAPITAL *must be constantly turning—locked up in slow lines it acts as a dead loss—reports show when it is producing at the highest rate possible.*

"Let every dollar of capital invested or borrowed perform its full duty," is the way a prominent banker expresses the need of keeping inventories, customers' accounts, notes receivable, cash and working liabilities at the minimum and at the same time producing the maximum earnings. These are conditions which the managers of a variety of concerns may look for in their statements. Just as records will show tendencies in sales and explain department outputs and machine efficiency, so the financial condition of a business may be watched.

Under normal conditions investment in working assets of such businesses as hardware, grocery, paint, shoes, jewelry, drug, dry goods, automobile and steel can easily be determined. Definite relationship must exist between capital represented in working assets and the annual turn-over. Records can be drawn from different sections of the business to show "lock-up in working capital" at the close of each month. Failure to keep this at the minimum necessitates borrowing and paying of interest otherwise unnecessary.

One manufacturer traced his uninvested working assets through his record of uncollected customers' accounts and inventories, as shown in Figure XI. Two branches, in St. Louis and Omaha, selling belting, pulleys and other supplies, did substantially the same volume of business and operated under much the same conditions. The figures showed, however, that the Omaha branch had an investment in stock and accounts $30,000 larger than that of the St. Louis branch. When the situation was sifted down to its elements, it was discovered that the Omaha branch did not give the same strict attention to stock keeping and the collection of accounts as did the St.

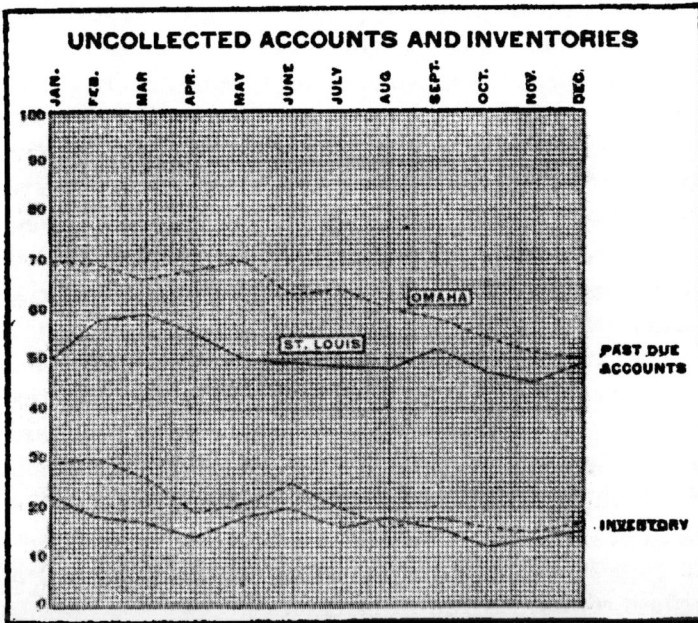

FIGURE XI: *Past due accounts and excessive inventories are difficult to control in many industries. By comparing his Omaha and St. Louis branches, a manufacturer of belting reduced his investment, as shown here on a scale of $1,000 units*

Louis office. By installing a perpetual inventory and efficient sales records and revising the collection methods, the Omaha situation was brought up to the St. Louis standard.

In like manner the investment in the several classes of assets in various businesses may be profitably compared. Just as well as in sales and expense, the head of the business may see his figures in a "per unit" form. On this uniform basis, the relative investment in different branches can be easily seen and the working assets kept at the lowest possible points in all.

Nor is it in the large business alone that this class of records is worth while. A printer doing an annual business of about $25,000, revised his storekeeping and accounting system and reduced his inventories by $1,500 and his uncollected customers' accounts by $2,000. This $3,500 has enabled him to pay off bank loans and save about $175 a year in interest. The plan by which he reduced his inventory should be of less interest to every business man than the fact that a basic principle in business is careful watch over the investment in inventories, customers' accounts, and notes receivable.

The inventory figure in any business is a worth while study, not only from the investment angle, but from that of sales and purchases. Comparisons of sales, purchases and inventory from time to time will bring out facts in the business and help to maintain their correct ratios. Records that show when to buy will enable the purchaser to keep fresh materials and stocks on hand, as well as reduce capital tied up in inventories.

That definite figures, rightly grouped, will bring before the head of a business a better understanding of his whole business, these various experiences of other managers show. Any business man may take a similar point of view on his figures.

Figures that prophesy mean the success or failure of men in business. For right accounting is more than history. It is not enough to know what has been done;

records should show what should be done. The directors of a large eastern manufacturing concern, with inventories valued at ten million dollars, voted to pay an expert eighteen thousand dollars a year to devise means of giving them figures that would prophesy. By devising and installing a system of purchasing, receiving and storekeeping that would enforce minimum stocks of raw materials, goods in process and finished products without impairing the efficiency of the business, the money tied up in inventories was reduced by nearly two million dollars. The directors proved the value of right accounting.

Any business man who looks upon his accounting as mere recording and not as a method of control for the details of his business misses the vital significance and use of the facts behind its figures.

❦

IT IS *the aim of every manufacturer to supply a better grade of goods at a lower price than the other fellow. This study to maintain a balance between grade and price revolves about the details. System is one of his greatest aids to this end.*

—Morris Selz
Founder, Selz, Schwab and Company

XVIII

GRAPHS THAT GUIDE
YOUR BUSINESS

By Kendall Banning

IN a small town up in the hills of New Hampshire is a small manufacturing plant that may properly be regarded as representative of its class. It employs about seventy-five people, operates a factory of moderate size and equipment, and, in its external aspects, does not differ materially from the thousands of small factories that are scattered throughout the country. Yet it maintains a department that might be considered in a measure as a complement to the "planning room" that is such an important factor in the Taylor system of shop management, and to it is credited a large part of the unusual efficiency that makes the factory conspicuous. For want of an authoritative term, this department is known as the "curve room."

It is the function of this curve room to keep graphic record of the activities of every phase of the business. This is done by means of charts, ranging from forms of ordinary size that may be kept in the correspondence files, to "graphs" the size of large wall maps, that are mounted on frames and operated similarly to the maps and drawings that are part of the equipment of nearly every large drafting office. Upon these graphs are kept annual, semi-annual, quarterly, monthly, weekly, daily and even hourly reports of the progress made by the departments, their costs, their output, their overhead costs, and the many detailed statistics that are needed to keep the executive heads of the plant in constant and accurate touch with each item of expense, sales and production. From the information thus tabulated, the management establishes standards by which the work of the factory is maintained, and is enabled to make provision for increases or decreases in the volume which it turns out by observing the "tendencies" as they appear, in picture form, on the various chart-reports.

GRAPHS *in office, store and factory are pictures of the figures, bringing out plainly the high and low spots in production—net results visualized.*

In a lesser degree, the graph is being used in many business offices—principally for indicating "tendencies" that serve as guides in making estimates. In the case of the present plant, however, over three hundred different records are kept by this map form. In some cases, two, three and even many more different but co-related records are kept on a single sheet for purpose of economy. The actual figures that serve as the basis for these graphs are, of course, kept in the files after the usual manner. While the graphs are accurate, and, so far as possible, show the detailed figures, they do not in all cases provide for the exact numbers, although they represent these figures and indicate where they may be found should more specific data than that which appears on the charts be required. While it is not probable that such an extensive use of graphs would be practical for every business, it is obvious that such a system for presenting records is of great value because of the opportunities for comparison with the corresponding periods of former years and months, that it makes possible.

In the case of this particular factory, the exact figures required for the maintenance of the various charts are gathered daily, and, in a few instances, at shorter intervals, by a clerk who is one of the staff of three employed in the curve room. The data in these reports are then transferred to the graphs in pencil form, or are "plotted in," to use the term of the drafting room. To insure accuracy in this work, one draftsman calls off the figures to his co-worker, who plots them in with pencil;

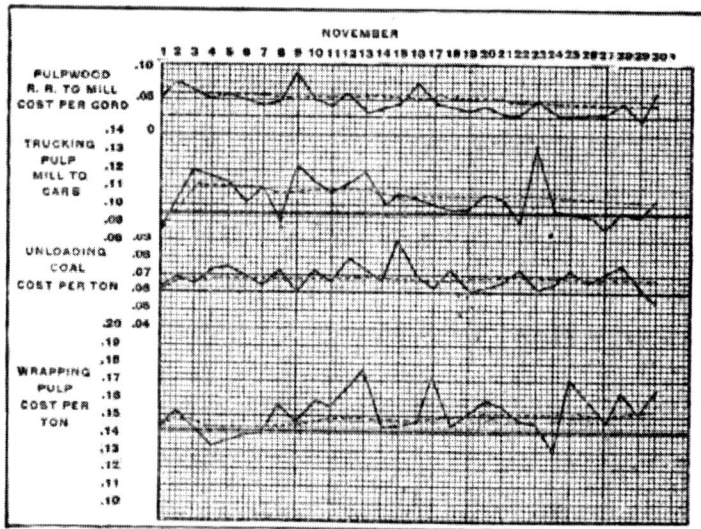

FIGURE XII: *This specimen section of a graphic map eight feet long shows, by means of colored lines, the actual daily costs, the average costs for the month and the "standard" cost*

the positions are then reversed and the process repeated, so that each man checks up the other's work. Twice a day the chief of the curve room goes over these charts and draws, in colored ink, the various lines that represent the figures that are required for record.

One of the most important features of this tabulating work, however, is the task of figuring out and charting the "average" and the "standard" lines, both of which are extensively used to serve as the basis of comparison. In Figure XII, for example, which shows a detail of one

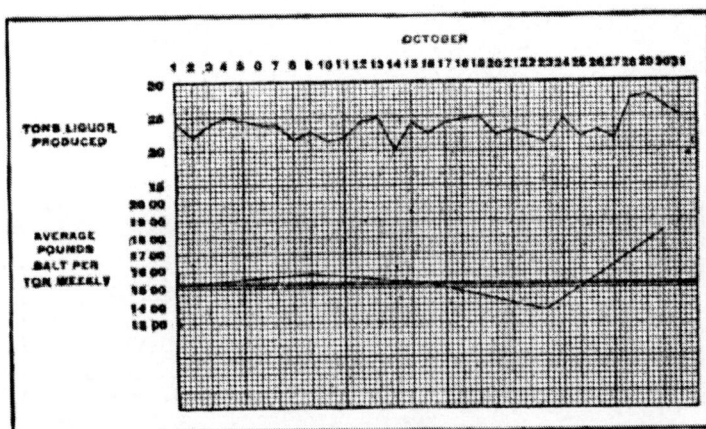

FIGURE XIII: On the "production" graphs are recorded significant data. This chart, for example, shows how many tons of liquor were produced and how many tons of salt were used

of the cost maps, the heavy broken lines indicate the actual costs of the items named in the space provided on the left, as recorded from day to day. The dotted lines that run through the daily cost lines indicate the monthly "average" of cost; in the original charts these monthly-average lines are further distinguished from the others by the use of red ink. These "average" cost lines are figured every day, in order to show clearly at any time the actual costs on any day as compared to the average for the month up to that point. But these statistics are given still greater value by indicating, by means of straight blue lines, the "standard" costs.

Thus the "actual," "average" and "standard" costs of each item of the business are shown in map form in such succinct and condensed way that any variation is made immediately apparent. When the activities of every de-

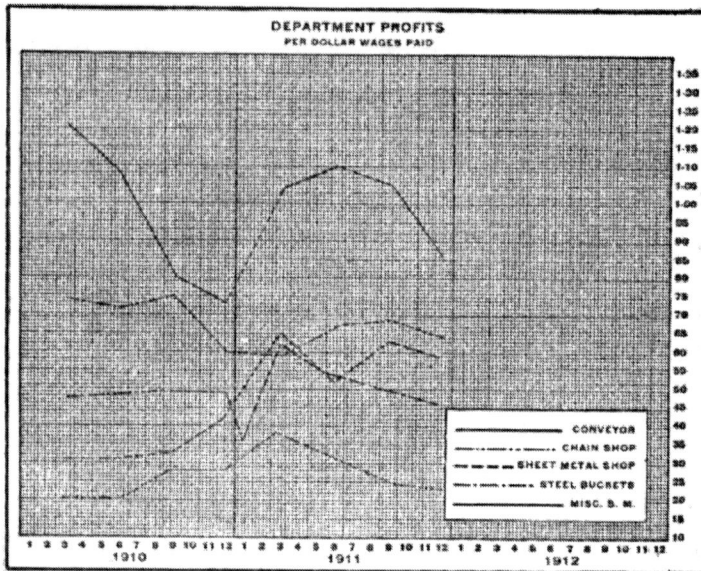

FIGURE XIV: The tendencies of "production" and "profit," as represented on this chart, are of great value in making up estimates for ensuing seasons

partment are similarly reduced to graphic form, it is a comparatively simple task for the management to keep in accurate touch with the progress of the plant by a daily visit to the curve room, where the records are kept ready of access.

Most of the charts are eight feet in length by about two feet in height—a size sufficient to contain a continuous daily curve for one year. They are mounted in wooden frames, after the manner familiar in architects'

and contractors' offices, and are suspended from the
ceiling.

These records are particularly useful in picturing the
output of a plant. In Figure XIII, for example, is illustrated the method by which the production of various
departments is tabulated both from day to day and from
week to week during the period of a month. The "average pounds salt per ton weekly" is indicated by a series
of straight lines that extend over weekly periods instead

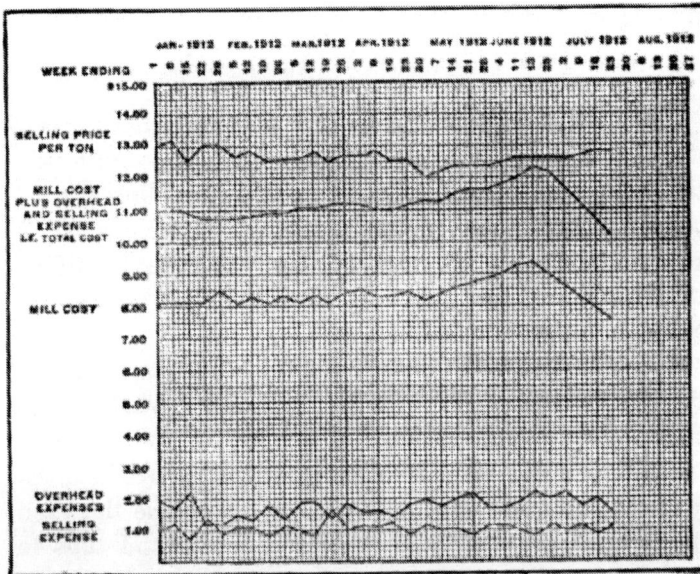

*FIGURE XV: With charts like this weekly "expense" graph, it is
possible to note digressions from the normal and detect leaks before they
assume large proportions*

of over daily periods by which the "tons liquor produced" is indicated at the top of the chart. The figures
which determine the make-up of these charts are collected every day from the factory, and upon these figures

the chart record is based. How these figures compare
with the standard production is indicated by the straight
line (on the original shown in blue) that is established
on the basis of former records.

Similarly, in Figures XIV and XV are represented
data that the management of the plant demands, and
that make evident many fluctuations that are not always
so apparent from the ordinary type of report that consists merely of comparative figures in parallel columns.

PRODUCTION *data of past years become standards
by which subsequent results are gauged—graphic
charts which set quotas and guide railway policies.*

It is obvious that such a system of tabulating records
is of especial value to the management in establishing
standards of work and of cost, and in providing for re-
current fluctuations of the markets. For instance, a
demand for the plant's product may vary with the different seasons of the year—a condition that would, of
course, be apparent on the graph.

From the records of past years, the management is enabled to determine the "quota" for each period and to
express this standard on the graph by means of a
straight blue line extending through the period in question. In the same way, it is possible to reduce the various costs of production to standard limits and thus to
check any undue excesses before they assume dangerous
proportions. It has been through these advantages that
the factory in New Hampshire has eliminated many of
the extravagances and wastes that mar the efficiency of
so many small plants, but which are usually uncorrected
merely through ignorance on the part of the management that any leaks exist. The use of such graphs is
valuable in warning the management of exceptional con-

ditions in the plant and in making it possible to provide for future conditions that, judging from the records of the past, may reasonably be expected.

Although used to advantage by all businesses, small as well as large, graphs have a peculiar value in concerns whose magnitude is such that the management is not in direct touch with all departments. A graphic picture in such cases forestalls the necessity of running with tedious care through long columns of figures, whose significance may even then be lost. Some of the leading railroads of the country have learned to make good use of the graph.

The principles and nearly all of the details of railway accounting are prescribed by the Interstate Commerce Commission. By law the railroads are required to follow the instructions of the Commission as to when, how, and what they shall report. The returns for expenses, however, are not so complete as the other figures, nor are they comparable between different railroads or different sections of the country because of striking differences in the division of traffic between passenger and freight, and differences in physical and operating conditions. The railroads have been left largely to their own initiative and resourcefulness, therefore, in developing a system for checking costs and utilizing their facilities and equipment.

One railroad in the East has developed the use of the graph to a state of high efficiency. Charts in this concern are prepared on thin paper so that blue prints may be made, and regularly each month as they are brought up to date, copies are furnished to the general and division officials. It has been found that the charts rouse a great interest in the returns and inspire keen rivalry between departments and divisions.

Figure XVI is a sample of the value of these charts.

It gives a bird's-eye view of the operation of a freight station employing sixty or seventy men and handling from one thousand to sixteen hundred tons of freight

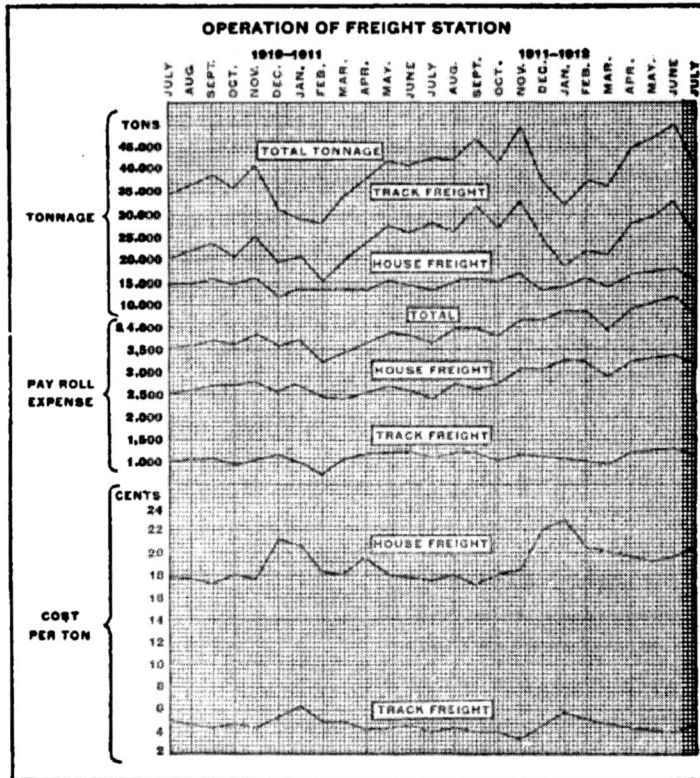

FIGURE XVI: This graph follows the monthly changes in the cost of operating a freight station. Compared with the outlay and results for preceding months and years, poor or efficient management shows up sharply

daily. At large stations the agent has each morning a memorandum statement showing the pay roll expense of the previous day, the tonnage handled, and the cost per ton. For every station, a monthly statement is prepared and "graphed," with a final graph summarizing the totals and general average for all freight stations.

. The facts in the operation of a yard where freight

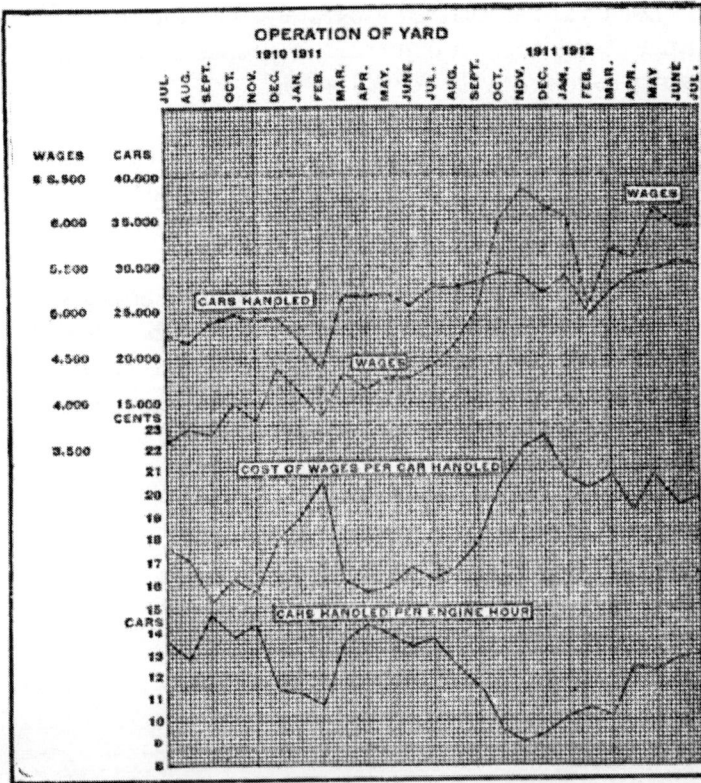

FIGURE XVII: *The startling pay roll advance, and the increase in labor and engine costs per car, after July, 1910, would normally be danger signals for the executive. The rise was really due to extensive terminal alterations*

trains are classified are shown in Figure XVII. The cost per car handled varies widely in different yards on account of the differences in facilities and the extent of the classification made necessary by the character of traffic and the location of the yard with respect to other divisions, junctions and connecting roads. The value of the statistics lies in comparing the current records of each yard with its record in previous months or previous years. Each yard is charted separately, but for the information of the officials one chart is prepared showing the results comparatively for all yards.

Other charts of a similar kind are prepared by this railroad and used with valuable results to show the conditions of operation in every department and division. The curves give instantaneous impressions. They make it possible for the mind to take in quickly a long series of related facts, and both the actual and relative changes in each when compared with the others and with different periods. Briefly, they give the maximum of information with the minimum of mental effort, and they are replete with corrective suggestion.

A SUCCESSFUL *man must know his business. He mus apply this knowledge—he must work, and he must work to the best advantage. And to work to the best advantage he must work with system.*

—John H. Converse

XIX

HOW TO CONTROL
EXPENSE ITEMS

By Edward L. Wedeles
Treasurer, Steele Wedeles Company

A N OFFICE boy earning three dollars a week once proposed an economy that saved our house a thousand dollars a year. He came to my desk and broached a plan that had never occurred to us: "Why can't we send acknowledgments by postal card, instead of by letter?"

At first there seemed to be objections to this method, chief of which was the publicity it might give to the affairs of merchants in small towns, but after we put the plan into operation we never had a complaint. We had been spending a thousand dollars a year for nothing.

Subsequently an idea occurred to us: "Why make any acknowledgment at all? All remittances reach us by check or draft, which the remitter gets back with our indorsement and the stamp of the bank through which it is paid. Isn't this enough?"

Again we changed our method, and since that time we have not sent out even the postal cards. Only in special instances do we now acknowledge remittances. Our customers understand, and our business goes just as smoothly as before, with the saving of a thousand dollars or more, not to mention the cutting off of a great volume of office work.

At another time we cut expenses materially by packing certain goods in cartons, instead of wooden boxes, as we had always done. A trial of the new method demonstrated that it not only reduced the expense, but gave just as much satisfaction, if, indeed, not more.

E*XPENSE analysis is an important part of the executive's duty—classification, tabulation and comparison aid him in locating hidden items of waste.*

So, all through the detail of a business, there is opportunity to analyze expense and cut it without disturbing the organization or the service to customers. New ideas may seem revolutionary at first and you are disinclined to adopt them. Often your only reason for failing to do so is purely sentimental. We had been paying a thousand dollars a year in postage largely from sentimental reasons, yet when we cut off this expense the sentiment vanished and no one seemed to care.

Initiative is just as necessary in handling expense as in selling goods. A man gets into a rut of expense and needlessly spends large sums because he does not look for a different way. Therefore, anything that will help him to think, will reduce expense. Anything that will keep expense items continually before him, will help him control this part of his business. He cannot always have a bright office boy to clip a thousand dollars here and there from the annual total, but he can always have graphic records to confront him and suggest the need. The more graphic the record, the more suggestive.

Expenses eat up a business unless controlled and checked. Money slips away easily in a thousand channels that never cease flowing. The demands on the cash-drawer are incessant. Unless there is vigilance, the expense outgo will exceed the income, and presently the drawer will be emptied.

.In every establishment there are two kinds of expense. On the one hand you have productive expense, which is the investment of money in salesmanship, labor, rent, advertising, and all those tangible and intangible commodities that go to make up the conduct of an establishment. It is an outgo that brings dividends, directly or indirectly. The principal items of productive expense may be likened to the parts of a machine; the smaller items are the oil that keeps the whole machine running smoothly.

On the other hand, you have expense which is waste, though it often masquerades under false colors. It is the money that gets away without bringing any return whatever. It is the drain that saps the life of a business and perhaps destroys it. Not always is this kind of expense easily detected, for it may be cleverly hidden. An incompetent or lazy employee may give in service less than he receives in salary; a team may be idle for a day; an advertisement may be poorly devised and cost more than it returns in business. These losses are more difficult to discover than the actual waste of some commodity that can be weighed or measured, but they are none the less non-productive expense.

To distinguish between these two varieties of expense, therefore, is important. To do so requires the exercise of the intellect in a double capacity; first, judgment; second, system.

The line of demarcation may be hard to find. For example, artificial light is a productive expense, because without it the transactions of store or office would cease. But just how much light is needed is a different question. Should there be ten, twenty or thirty lamps? Can two use the same light? These are matters to be determined by the judgment, not by bookkeeping or statistics. Eyesight, health, efficiency, are all to be considered. No mathematics will determine for you just where the light bill ceases to be a productive expense and becomes non-productive.

But take the two electric light meters, each supplying the same number of lamps under the same conditions,

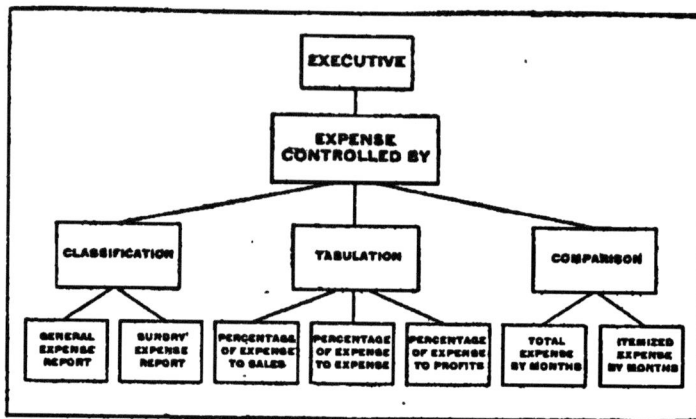

FIGURE XVIII: This chart shows how expense once it is classified can be supervised and controlled by means of comparative reports

and let one show double the expense of the other in a given period. The question is no longer one of judgment, but of system. Indeed, it must be system itself that discovers for you this very wasteful expense. You may have the best judgment in the world on all matters involving business logic, but if you have an inadequate expense system the drain on the cash-drawer will go unchecked.

A satisfactory system by which a managing executive may watch and control the expense of his establishment involves three things: classification, tabulation, comparison. These make up the means of discovering the leaks in expense, so far as ink and paper can show them.

In classification, it is scarcely possible to go too much into detail. The modern tendency is to divide and subdivide expense outgo until there is no possibility of classifying it further. It is only through these minute classifications that tabulation and comparison have their full value. For example, take the electric light meters just referred to. Suppose no individual record was kept of each meter, but all were charged against one general account, light. The waste would go on undetected. Carry the illustration further. Suppose that individual records were kept of each meter, but not tabulated. Or suppose, again, that the meters were all classified separately and tabulated, but no one made the comparison. These three elements, you see, are vitally connected one with another.

*C*LASSIFICATION *of all expenses so that the untagged items are insignificant—this is the basis of any satisfactory system of controlling them.*

I believe it possible to classify business expense to the point where the untagged items are almost infinitesimal. In our own business we classify and tabulate ninety-nine and eight-tenths per cent of expenses.

Expense items reach my desk daily in the form of entries in two books which classify general expense and sundry expense. These books are ruled like a double-column journal, but are divided into accounts like a ledger, a certain number of pages being set apart for each classification of expense. A bookkeeper posts these books from the general cash book, entering items in the left-hand column, and in the body of the page a full identification or explanation of the item.

The accounts are arranged alphabetically, and indexed.

The classified and general expense accounts are as follows:

Advertising, including only general advertising not subject to classification against particular brands of goods

Agencies, embracing reports of all kinds on customers

Attorneys' fees and court costs

Brokerage, including travelers' salaries at branches

Teaming done by teams other than our own

Charity, covering contributions to institutions and the like

Cost books, or daily price sheets sent to travelers

Fuel

Fixtures and tools, including office furniture, alterations in partitions or railings, and smaller tools and appliances, such as hammers, saws, etc.   Larger apparatus and implements, such as typewriters and adding machines, are charged to property accounts

Insurance

Light

Mail order department

Meals, embracing expenses of employees working overtime

Office salaries, covering wages of every kind except those in the shipping department, which are charged to sundry salaries

Power

Postage

Rent

Sundry salaries

Stationery

Sundries, unclassified in this book

Taxes

Teaming, by our own wagons

Telegrams

Telephone

Travelers' salaries, including those of buyers, department managers and the officials who control them.   In our business we have no account directly representing travelers' traveling expenses, for we allow our travelers a given sum to cover both salary and expense.

At the close of each month the totals from these classified expense accounts are transferred to a book which records comparative expenses. This book is ruled like a trial-balance sheet, so that the various items are arranged in tables for comparison month by month. These monthly totals in turn, are classified by years and arranged for comparison.

The sundry expenses are minutely subdivided and include the smallest items of expense; even showing a record of matches and soaps, and tickets purchased from persons soliciting for entertainments. The totals from the Sundry Expense book are, of course, included in the tabulated recapitulations in the "Comparative Expense Books."

These books are valuable as a medium for the methodical scrutiny of daily items. From them you can watch the outgo in all its details and ramifications. Expense may be compared to a group of water-courses draining some common region. The streams flow in every direction, all of them centering at the same source. Some of them are only rivulets, some creeks, some rivers, but all drawing away the same waters. To get a birds-eye view of this group of streams, you must mount an eminence. To attempt to follow each separately would be a long and tedious task, but from an elevation you may study the course of every one.

So, too, you can scan the expense streams from the eminence of your own desk if you have the proper system. No rivulet will be too small to see. Each entry will be itemized under its proper classification. In running through the accounts every morning you can place your finger on items that appear too large, or uncalled for, or which need explanation. You can point out the spots where expense streams must be dammed.

Expense is best controlled by centralizing its supervision. Subject all its ramifications to some system that reduces them to this daily scrutiny at your desk. And, necessarily, condense all the items as far as is compatible with this minute classification. Have your expense records permanent, in the form of books, for the detached report sheet is bulky and inconvenient to handle. The most efficient record lies in your private account books.

R EDUCTION *of expenses to a percentage basis puts them all on the same level—then the wastes and discrepancies appear at once in glaring outlines.*

But the classified and comparative books named make up only one step in the controlling of expense. They give you a daily, monthly and yearly scrutiny, but their statistical value is as yet imperfect. Their figures represent money, not percentages. In keeping the various items of expense at their proper ratio, percentage statistics play an important role. The more detailed these statistical tables are, the more efficient will be your supervision of outgo. The deadly parallel is used here, not to show similarities, but to reveal incongruities, dissimilarities. Expense, as a rule, is governed by fixed or progressive percentages. When there are abrupt variations from this rule, they must be shown up conspicuously on the records. Nothing does this so graphically as percentage tables.

For this purpose we keep a number of books, made up of tabulated percentages, monthly and yearly.

The first gives the percentage of expense to sales. The page is ruled at the left for entering the various classifications, one under another; at the right are perpendicular columns for the percentages. Thus the table shows Office Expense, Salaries, Sundry Salaries, Cartage, and the like. If, for example, you desire to know the ratio of office expense to sales, turn to the index, find the table, and run your finger along the designated crossline; you can see at a glance the percentages for each month in the year. Turning to the yearly table, you can compare the years in the same way as the months.

Going down a line, you follow the ratio that salaries bear to sales, and so on through all the subdivisions pertaining to the expense of selling.

The advantage of this record is manifest. All these items bear a natural relationship to the chief classification under which they are grouped—Sales. For example, once you have determined approximately the percentage office expense ought to bear to sales, you have the key to the subsequent controlling of this item. The ratio may have to be increased gradually because of increased costs, but if you do increase it you do so intelligently. You know exactly why. You do not waste brain force wondering why your selling expense is so big or where you ought to cut. The percentage table shows you just what department is beyond its normal ratio.

The second comparative percentage book shows the ratio of expense to expense. In other words, it shows the ratio each item of expense bears to the total expense.

This book is ruled the same as the other, following out the monthly and yearly percentages in the same manner. For instance, suppose you want to learn what relation your teaming bears to the total cost of conducting your business. You wish to establish some rule for controlling this item. The percentage rule is an excellent guide. Month by month, year by year, tabulate your teaming expense in ratios. Without such a table, you must go it blind. There will be wastes you can not detect.

In this book it is scarcely necessary to tabulate with extreme minuteness. The minor classifications detailed in the more general expense books may be omitted and only the larger classifications tabulated. But this book affords opportunity to keep track of expense percentages in any general or special item the executive desires. Every business has its particular departments or phases especially in need of watching.

The third comparative percentage book gives the ratio of expense to gross merchandise profits. The method of tabulation is the same as already described. Here, too, the classifications need not be so detailed as in the daily and monthly itemized record of expenses.

COMPARATIVE *statistics books may be multiplied as far as necessary, giving the important facts about every big and little phase of the business.*

This book gives you a succinct survey of the bearing the expense account has upon the business as a whole. It measures the difference between income and outgo, and shows in percentages the results of the firm's enterprises. If the ratios shown are too large to harmonize with the amount of capital invested, the various classifications may be analyzed and traced back in ever-increasing detail to the tabulated dollars and cents tables and accounts.

In addition to these important books of statistics, we have others of local value. Thus, there is a book devoted to electric light and elevator meters. It is ruled for statistical tables. Each meter has a column running the vertical way of the page, and in each cross-space is entered the sum charged against that meter for a given month, in dollars and cents. A full column represents the total paid on a given meter for a year. So, passing your finger from left to right across the page, you can follow the history of any elevator by its meter, month by month, checking its performance.

Another book useful to firms having teams is that containing statistics of the stable. It is ruled to give the quantities of feed consumed and the cost. Take oats, for example. The table shows the number of bushels used daily and monthly, the average daily cost, and the average cost per bushel. The hay table shows the same statistics in tons. So, too, are tabulated the daily number of horses consuming this feed, and the daily average of horses. If you watch this stable book you will quickly detect and control non-productive outgo. Once you know the proper average quantity of feed required per horse, any over-feeding, under-feeding, or waste, must be discovered.

This system of recording and watching expense may be extended indefinitely and made as general or specific as the needs of your business require. The books and tables described may be reduced to three or multiplied into a score, and each will reveal in undeniable figures the trend of some department or classification of your business.

📖

MANUFACTURERS *are showing renewed interest in production costs. For here is something every manager can control. Market and selling conditions may be outside his definite control. He can buy right—sometimes. He can put over a special selling campaign. But more and more he must study production costs and know that they are exactly right.*

—J. Eddy Chace

XX

MAKING CLERICAL WORK AUTOMATIC

By H. M. Wood
Of the Lodge & Shipley Machine Tool Company

AN executive in our plant need not wait two weeks to know the cost of a job that was done the day before. If, for example, he wishes to know the cost of the one hundred headstocks used in one lot of eighteen-inch lathes, all the cost department has to do is assemble a series of cost cards, find the assembly group number corresponding to this style of headstock and run these cards through a machine. Records which, under some conditions, might take two weeks to assemble because of the clerical work necessary in posting and compiling the data, can be turned out in a day in this way.

Primarily this speed in handling cost figures is made possible by the use of an assorting machine similar in general construction to the machines used by the United States Census Bureau. While this machine does much of the laborious posting and calculating which otherwise would have to be done by accountants, the method of handling labor and material records in the factory is an essential element in the success of the system. In the first place, in order that records of work and costs may be assembled in compact form, the plant as a whole is organized on the numerical basis. Departments, men, machines, operations and materials are all numbered. All the work and the operations are standardized and

identifying numbers given to each. There are numbers
for standard parts, for repairs, tools, new parts, and so
on. Consequently, when a job number is given to an
order that number in itself is a key which identifies the
job in several different ways.

MACHINES *and methods that simplify the analysis
of cost figures in the office and bring the big facts
quickly and accurately to the executive's desk.*

How this system of numerical identification is worked
out and how it simplifies the handling of clerical detail
can be well illustrated by analyzing the method of finding the cost of one part of one lot of eighteen-inch lathes.
On this lot it is, of course, necessary to keep distinct
records of labor and material; to know how much time
each man spends on each operation; what machine he
uses. This part headstock of the eighteen-inch lathe belongs to the assembly part known as a group by the number 55. The part has a piece number 1,100 which designates the main headstock casting and it has the shop job
number, 14,450 which keys it as belonging to a lot of one
hundred eighteen-inch lathes. The material and time
for this number are charged against the shop number
and the piece number.

Requisitions for material are made upon the stock
department in the usual way and the record of material
used is kept by the stock keepers and forwarded by
them to the cost department.

The labor on this part is kept on a time sheet which is
filled out by a timekeeper who visits each machinist
periodically and keeps track of his time in a loose-leaf
book with pages ruled like Form I.

As this form shows, when these time sheets and the
material sheets are turned in to the cost department, the

data on them is in the form of numbers and is really an analysis of these numbers, each of which identifies some bit of cost information.

Formerly the cost department posted time from the time sheets to a book at the end of the week and classified the results in columns under individual headings. Now instead of posting, the data from the time book is assembled compactly on a card like that shown in Form II.

All the data pertaining to time keeping and to stock keeping is assembled by punching small, round holes in the proper location on the card shown in Form II for the time and Form III for the material. Take the analysis of the time on job number 14,450, piece number 1,100 as an example. The first three columns show the date and all the cards of the same day are punched simultaneously by a gang punch, on that day. In the card shown (Form II), the figure 3 punched in the first column indicates the third month of the year which itself is keyed by the punch mark in the figure 10 at the top of the second column. The punch mark at figure 3 indicates that this operation was performed the third week in the month and in the third column the figure 14 (one punch for each figure) is a key to the day of the month.

Each department, numbered consecutively, is easily identified on the form by the punched marks, and the two punched marks in the fourth column indicate that the work was performed in department 10, the planer department.

The fifth column with three punch marks shows that the workman whose number is 222 is a machinist to whom the time on this job is to be charged.

In the next main sub-division under the title "Charge" is punched the job number 14,450, which is a key to the

FORMS I, III and IV: *The time sheet at the back is filled out by a clerk who visits the men at their work. The front and middle cards are the stock keeper's and the "census" records of materials used* lot of one hundred eighteen-inch lathes. The punch mark on the left side of this same column shows that this particular job is a standard part and as such is distinguished from repairs, tools, and so on, which are designated by name in this subdivision of the column headed "charge."

The piece number 1,100 designates the main headstock casting, and the group number 55 is the numerical way of stating that this particular lot of parts is one belonging to the complete headstock number 55. The name of the operator planing the bottom of the headstock, expressed in arithmetical terms, is 134. The department and the part have already been designated, and this separate classification of operations is necessary to show the specific portion of the casting which is being planed. Similarly, the machine in the department numbered 1234 means that the work was done on the thirty-six-inch planer.

The columns for hours, indicating elapsed time and the amount paid, are shown in the next two columns. The amount paid is the wage charge against this particular job. It is, of course, calculated in the cost department by multiplying the time on the job taken from the time sheet (Form I) and multiplied by the man's rate. The wage charge is indicated by the punch marks in the column headed "Amount."

In the last column on Form II the character of the work from the accounting standpoint is designated. The abbreviations in this column refer to overhead, non-productive, productive, and so on. The punch mark indicates that this work is productive labor.

Store room records of material are kept in just the same way. Two sets of cards, similar in design to that shown in Form III, are used for keeping the material records. Green cards are used for material coming in from the foundry and pink cards for material coming in from the machine shop receiving office. The record of goods received from the foundry is indicated by marks punched directly on the card, just as the time records are kept.

A monthly summary of the totals of the records of both green and pink cards is tabulated on a white card marked store room (Form IV).

So in compact shape a vast amount of information regarding the details of time and material charges is available. The next step is to assemble and analyze these

FORM II: Holes are punched in this card by a machine. They are then run through another machine which assorts them so that any desired statistics can be secured

charges. For this work the "census-machine" is used. After the cards have been punched they are thrown promiscuously into a box with others and when all the cards for the day are prepared they are run through the assorting machine and distributed according to groups.

The assorting machine has pockets numbered from 0 to 9, thus corresponding to the figures in the columns on the cards.

A scale on the machine is graduated in such a way

that it corresponds exactly to the location of the vertical columns on the cards. A brush is adjustable to any position along the scale and in its different positions it makes electrical contact with a small revolving shaft. To assort a group of cards for any particular column, it is only necessary to set the brush over that column on the scale and feed the cards into the machine, which automatically sorts them at the rate of two hundred and sixty per minute.

A SSORTING *punched cards by means of electric tabulation to find any desired set of statistics saves a large amount of clerical work in getting costs.*

Take the time cards on our lathe part as a sample. In the first place, the machine is set for the right-hand column and the package of miscellaneous cards is thus separated into the various classifications of labor. Selecting the productive group, these cards are again run through the machine and standard parts and labor parts are separated, these two being the only subdivisions of productive labor.

Then the time on this particular lot of eighteen-inch lathes will be turned in on standard parts, and if the "standard" subdivisions of "productive" labor are run through the machine again, they may be assorted according to job or "charge" numbers.

This takes a little longer, as the charge number consists of five figures. For the first time the machine is set to give nine piles assorted by tens of thousands. The brush is then set over one notch to the right on the indicator scale, and all the numbers in the first ten thousand are assorted into nine piles of thousands. By similar successive set-overs the subdividing is carried through hundreds, tens and units.

This leaves the cards in numerical order according to the "Charge" numbers, with all cards of a given "Charge" number together. The cards are then placed in files provided for the purpose, with index cards separating the different "Charge" numbers. Cards for "Charge" number 14,450 remain in this file until our lot of eighteen-inch lathes is completed.

When this lot of lathes is finished and the cards are all in, all of the cards now filed under "Charge" number 14,450 are run through an adding machine. This machine automatically foots up the totals of hours and wage costs for the entire job directly from the punch marks on the cards. These totals from the adding machine are then "posted" into permanent records, and the cards are replaced in their file to await calls for further information.

When there is much data to be assembled the advantages of this system are apparent. For some of the information on the cards there may never be any call. But the cards are filed under the "Charge" numbers and the more detailed data is not worked up until something specific is required.

If, for example, the cost of the one hundred head-stocks used in eighteen-inch lathes is wanted, all that is necessary to do is to run through the machine all of the "Charge 14,450" cards so as to pick out "Group 55." Then add up the amounts to get the wage cost.

On the other hand, if you wish to find how long a certain machine tool worked on this lot, assort all the "Charge 14,450" cards by the machine column and add the number of hours on the cards which assemble themselves under the machine number wanted.

The assorting and adding machines effect a great saving of labor in your cost department, since you need fewer and cheaper clerks.   There is less chance for errors because when once the cards are properly punched, the machines are bound to do the work correctly.   But the most important consideration of all is the speed with which you get your results; under this system you can have the cost of a lot the day following completion, whereas under other methods it would take a week or so to post the records and compile the data.

𝕄

ALMOST every large concern that started twenty years ago and is successful today, could today duplicate that success. You can be a Wanamaker, a Marshall Field, or an Altman, if you personally attend to your store, look after your window displays, watch your business and study it thoroughly. You can become successful just as easily as these big men have done before. It depends upon how you study your business and how much you love your business.

—Samuel Brill
President, Brill Brothers

Lightning Source UK Ltd.
Milton Keynes UK
UKOW020734241012

201102UK00003B/22/P

9 781147 549478